FIND YOUR FIRE

FIND YOUR FIRE

**STORIES AND STRATEGIES TO *INSPIRE*
THE CHANGEMAKER INSIDE YOU**

Terri Broussard Williams
Movement Maker Publishing

First paperback edition, March 27, 2020

Cover design by Jennifer Pace Duran
Interior editing and design by BMcTALKS Press
Formatting by Tamara Cribley, The Deliberate Page

Library of Congress Control Number: 2020904681

ISBN 978-1-7341595-0-9 (paperback)
ISBN 978-1-7341595-1-6 (ebook)

www.TerriBWilliams.com

This book is dedicated to #Firestarters around the world. You are enough. You are smart. You are valuable. You are kind. You are powerful. Your time is now—so show up. What you create with faith and fortitude will change the world!

To Jan Coussan and Janeen Robin, heaven's newly acquired angels, who both passed away in 2019.

Table of Contents

Acknowledgments

You might have heard me say "No movement moves alone." I have to thank everyone who has helped me build this movement over the past two years: Root+River, Pace Creative, WISH SEO, Ty West, Shift Creatives, and Brassy Broadcasting Network. You never said "no" to any of my crazy ideas or short deadlines.

There was a krewe that made me better and believed in me times infinity. In no particular order, I thank Erin Lockard, Angelica Rodriguez, Breezy Ritter, Kara Factor, Amanda Moore, Sarah Beckham, Jeff Beckham, Jen Duran, Scott James, Shana Burg, and Tamara Cribley. They let me call audibles when needed. Each of you only wanted me to succeed and never asked for anything in return. You are now my family!

To those that are helping me look toward the future, including Punchline Speakers and Pioneering Collective, let's get this show on the road! And to all of my professors and classmates at the University of Pennsylvania School of Social Policy and Practice. The conversations, assignments, and even the required readings provided clarity for me during my time of writing and reminded me of how I wanted to show up in the world.

My blog is called #MovementMakerCollective for a reason. There's a huge collective of interns that keep this movement moving, and these incredibly talented young women are future #Firestarters in their own right: Peyton Short, Victoria Cates, and Tatiana Gonzales-Quiroga. Shout-out to Katie Goldstein who helped us tie loose ends in our early days!

Not many people know this, but when I was in elementary school, my mother made me read as punishment. I never admitted that I loved reading because it was a glorious punishment. That love turned into a desire to volunteer for nearly five years at the Lafayette Public Library. Thank you for giving me the opportunity to flip through books when I should've been shelving them. I learned the possibilities of the world in your four walls.

There are five women who molded me probably more than they realized:

- The first was my 4-H agent, Jan Coussan. Mrs. Jan, as we called her, was my coach for demonstration projects, teaching me poise and to never to be afraid of a crowd. She was there the first time I gave a speech in public and told me it would serve me later in life.

- Janine Robin was my very last Girl Scouts troop leader. Mrs. Janine always told me how much I inspired her. I never quite understood as a high schooler how I might inspire an adult, but I do realize today that this is a much-needed superpower in movement-building.

- Maria Pitre was my high school speech coach. Miss Pitre pushed me to do better and forced me to enter the oratory competition as well as extemporaneous speaking.

- Lori Fresina saw me at a time when I thought no one did. She reminded me that I was an influencer and that if I ever felt like I wasn't moving the needle to remember that so many people were looking up to me because I *was* moving it. And, gosh darn it, she taught me how to power map. That skill is priceless!

- Fayruz Benyousef helped me see my power in my adult years by showing me the data behind my ability to light a crowd. I'm not sure I'd ever have believed her if she hadn't shown me the numbers. But that moment changed the course of my life.

I must acknowledge the many male mentors I've had in my career. They've taught me the ways of Capitol buildings, shown me tough love, and treated me no differently than their brothers. It is because of three in particular that I am the lobbyist and, quite honestly, the person I am today.

To the #Firestarters in this book, I've watched you in some tough situations. I've watched you lead. I know your heart. I see you. Thank you for the work you do on behalf of women everywhere. You lead with grace and great intention. I give you mad props.

I'm a graduate of Louisiana State University, and my time as a Tiger helped me to see just how big the world is and gave me just the right push to figure out how I would show up in it. I'm currently a student at the University of Pennsylvania. Penn has helped me put words to the things I've experienced as a professional, giving me the framework for much of what you've read in my book.

To my friends and FRamily—There are so many of you to name and so many of you to thank. It wasn't until I met my FRamily that I understood that I was worthy of much more than a career, that I had a gift that was bigger than just me. It wasn't until I met my FRamily that I learned the "universe moves at the speed of relationships," and I had so many relationships I could move FAST! My friends have put up with me the past two years as I've gone from "I think I want to have a blog" to "I want to record videos and write a book." No one told me I was crazy, and everyone offered to help however they could. Natalie, Michelle, Jenna, Hannah H., Rebecca, Larissa, Erika, Vanessa, Naomi, Darie, Afra, Heather, Dena, Hannah N., Stacy, Courtney, Tamaria, Virgina, Kesha, Annie, Debbie R., and Violet—Thank you for being the first to read something, listen to me cry about how much work I had to do, or encourage me to keep plugging along.

Dee, Stephanie, and Wendy—As they say, what doesn't kill us makes us stronger. Who cares about goals and excellent or skilled ratings? The only goal I have these days is to be the Spice Girls with you! Thank you for being the women behind the hype text during my transition. I never told you, but those texts were what I needed to jump.

Tammy and Midge—When I asked for a million dollars to start a movement, you never flinched. You figured out a way to move mountains (and pennies) to save lives. And you also knew I would figure out the way to get out of my own way.

What got you here won't get you there, right?

Jill—You recognized talent in me when I was a stubborn, young lobbyist who only wanted to win. You would always tell me to "fight another day," helping me realize that impact is more than just a "w" on the scoreboard.

Eboni—You're younger, but you're definitely a big sister to me! Ladylike and a boss with integrity while wearing pearls, you reminded me just how much I'm worth and that I can do anything unapologetically while being #PrettyPowerful.

My mentees, Candace, Maria, Chelsi, and Ashley—I learn from *you* each and every time we speak. Who else is going to loan me a light ring for, like, a year?

Angela, my executive coach, is incredible. When I told her I couldn't pay her because my nest egg had to go to this project, she said no payment was due because she believed in me. I have no words for the kindness you have shown to me and the gift you have given me.

There are so many people that have helped shaped me, including my AHA buddies, Blogger buddies, Austin Dream Team, NGen Co-Hort, #AmExLeads family, StartingBloc, The Fab Four,

Godiva Chocolates, my DC and Socrates friends, REALITY family, Lobbyist Conference compadres, Lafayette Ladies, Champagne Caucus, Wine Camp Crew, Church on the Move, and the infamous Trustee Board. I don't know leaders who are more exceptional, more loyal, and who more consistently show up when needed. And, most importantly, you show me love.

#MovementMakerCollective—Yes, you! There are so many of you who reply to my posts or send me DMs and ideas. When I began this work, I didn't know if there would be an audience. I wasn't too sure anyone would care. It wasn't until someone told me they followed me at a Washington, DC reception that I understood the power of telling MY story. You showed up, and you continue to do so today.

To the Broussard, Dugas, Biagas, Bourg, Cormier, Lemelle, Louis, Parker, and Harris families—Thank you. You've helped this awkward, talkative, strong-willed child become the person she was meant to be. And I owe you forever.

To my grandparents, Novella and Alton Dugas and Margaret and Daughty Broussard—You are the engines in my work. At a time when people of color didn't have much, you understood what it took to make things work. And you understood that the underpinnings of life were the things that made you strong and the things that gave you hope.

Lemuel and Brent—You are so much alike. I'm lucky to have a cheering squad of men who believe in me and consistently place me before themselves. You have big hearts, a desire to help others and wanderlust—and I strive to be more like you both. Thank you for balancing me out and reminding me that it's OK to not have a deadline. It's OK to just live!

Pete—My heart still feels hollow when I think you'll never be able to pick up this book and read it. I miss our daddy-daughter dates to B. Dalton's to pick out books and calling you to talk about the injustices in the world. P.S. Can you see the 2019 LSU Tigers football team from heaven?

Carole—I use the words "faith and fortitude" to describe the values I learned from our family. They were always associated with you. You're the first #Firestarter I knew: the one who never backs down, the one who figures out a way. Mom, I admire every ounce of you, and I love you.

Foreword

Finding your fire, or inner driving energy, doesn't happen overnight. I first tapped into mine during medical school at Washington University. My immigrant parents had told me that the only way they would finance my education was if I became a physician. It took a lot of hard work, but I was dedicated to living up to their dreams, not my own. Once I got into medical school, a tiny voice kept nagging that I wasn't where I was supposed to be. That voice led me to my own dream of pursuing a career in the financial sector. Dropping out of medical school is one of the biggest risks I have ever taken. My family was unhappy, and I had to face disappointing a lot of people.

This story leads us to a very important question we all need to answer: How do we tap into the unique fire we all possess and use it to live a life of purpose and passion? You need patience to see the fruits of the decisions you make when you listen to your inner voice. In my journey, I hit early speed bumps. Instead of jumping fully into the world of numbers and analysis, I applied for healthcare analyst jobs, thinking it was a happy medium between the world I had just left and the new one I wanted to create for myself. There's nothing like a few false starts to test your mettle or your faith in your intuition.

When I finally made the jump to finance, I was so passionate about my work that my career took off. Passion fueled by your inner voice creates good work. I worked at two large banks and landed a job as a controller at an $8B hedge fund. I ultimately became one of the youngest chief financial officers on Wall Street, growing the fund from $90M to $500M over two years.

I truly found my fire when I jumped with both feet into mission-driven work. That inner voice grew from a whisper that I (mostly) heeded into confident, unwavering intuition. I made my first passion move since dropping out of med school when I left Wall Street for a telemedicine startup dedicated to ensuring people had 24/7 access to a medical expert.

While working in healthcare, I was struck by how male-dominated it was. Women were the biggest consumers yet the most underrepresented in healthcare leadership. I wanted to change that, so I co-founded HealthTech Women New York to empower women in the healthcare industry to lead and innovate.

Then that voice resurfaced in the form of a question: How could I bring together my finance skills and my experience in tech entrepreneurship to help drive change in the nonprofit world? I had noticed that the sector seemed particularly risk-averse, held back by antiquated ways of thinking and doing. I wanted to shake things up. This led me to the Association of Junior Leagues International Inc. (AJLI), a 115-year-old nonprofit organization that empowers and trains women to catalyze change in their communities.

I met Terri at an association board meeting. Immediately, I was blown away by the inspiring leadership she brought to the table. After several extremely rewarding years at AJLI, I have moved on to a new role where my experience and passion help my work make a global impact. As chief financial officer at Charity: Water, I have never been more content professionally than I am now, and I owe that to listening to my gut and finding (and nurturing) my fire.

A year ago, I gave a talk to emerging leaders at Harvard University and shared my journey from disappointing my parents by dropping out of med school to where I am now, living *my* dream and not someone else's. Many young women came up to me afterward, asking me how I had gathered the courage to do what I truly wanted despite pressure from family and society. They wanted to know how they could become disrupters, change makers, artists, entrepreneurs, dancers—radically different things than what their family expected of them.

I was very surprised that young women today still face the same challenges that I had hoped would become obsolete. The truth, though, is that women will always need to find our fire. Growing up, societal cues encourage us to be submissive. When we take risks and follow our gut, we are all too often told that we are falling out of step, swerving out of our lane. To me, finding your fire is about owning who you are and what you are, about growing that tiny voice into one so loud it can never be drowned out.

The stories in Terri's book are about women who listened to that voice—their gut instinct—and then let it grow louder and louder. What started as their individual, internal revolutions led to much broader societal impact. The more you tap into that inner fire and let it mature, the more you will succeed and be inspired by it.

I hope these stories inspire you, the way they have me, to think about how to nurture that inner fire even more—even if it means defying parents, taking big financial risks, standing up to big business or fighting for what you believe in, even if it is controversial. Finding your fire will always lead you to bigger and better things.

Here's to all of us on the journey of finding and nurturing that inner fire. It is incredibly exciting to think about what the future holds as more women find and grow that fire. I am so honored to be part of Terri's incredible project to help more women ignite change, and I can't wait to hear the stories of the readers whose paths change course as a result of reading this book.

Sincerely,
Aditi Deeg
Chief Financial Officer, Charity: Water

A Letter to Firestarters

This is a book for anyone who wants to be inspired by those who are already leading change. The stories that form the heart and soul of the book are from women who have found the courage, grace, and fortitude to take bold action in the face of daunting odds. Like Angie Provost, who left Houston for rural Louisiana to rediscover her connection to the land and carry the mantle of her family's agricultural legacy. Or Amanda Edwards, our mutual friend who ran in the Democratic primary in hopes of becoming the first African American US senator for Texas. While Amanda didn't make the run-off, I bet she says that the race helped her find her own fire.

Working with servant leaders like Stacey Abrams and Cecile Richards, I've learned something from them that I hope you will see in the pages of this book: Leading is as much about how you win as it is about how you live your life even when you've lost an election, your job, your farm. Let this book inspire you whether you're on top or you've hit a stumbling block. It will resonate for you no matter where you are in life.

It is such an honor to be a part of my sister Terri's first book, *Find Your Fire*. And what a book it is. It represents everything that brought us together four years ago when we met at a collective for Black professionals. We bonded immediately over our shared desire to see more women succeed professionally and have been friends, supporters-in-chief, and sounding boards for each other ever since.

This book is the fruit of many years of hard work and determination for Terri, and you will see it on every page you read. The book is a huge milestone in the work she began two years ago when she started the Movement Maker Collective, her multimedia platform to help people lead change and ignite movements. I remember messaging her when she started her website and her blog to tell her "I see you" and that I loved what she was doing by creating a space to uplift women. I continue to admire everything that she does, and this book is a part of that admiration.

I would have especially benefited from a book like *Find Your Fire* during my first two years of college—when you would have been hard-pressed to find more than a handful of women leaders in my state. At that age, I wasn't involved in creating change or leading or movement building because I didn't yet have the confidence, and I didn't see enough women that looked like me in positions of leadership and authority. Now, I can't imagine what my life would have been like if I hadn't gotten involved. I wake up every single day and live my passion for politics and for getting women politically and civically engaged. It's scary to think that fear could have kept me from doing what I love. Hearing about women leaders and their journey would have moved me from the sidelines to engagement much earlier. For me, this book is an investment in the future of women, especially women of color. It's another way this generation is holding the door wide open for future generations of young women—because we see you.

Just as much as this would have been a wonderful book for my younger self, it is also a fabulous one for me today. When you're watching television, walking through the bookstore, or paging through magazines, it is still rare to see leaders and entrepreneurs who are women. When we look at movement-building, so much of it is still done by men. So many of our families do not have roots in entrepreneurship, business, or politics. We are self-made, and we grow from those who charted the path before us. It is important for me to hear about the leadership journeys of other women to get ideas and to learn how to be better at the things I'm doing now.

So no matter why you pick up *Find Your Fire*, I hope its pages spark something in you: maybe the courage to take that leap of faith and start your own movement or maybe if you are like my eighteen-year-old self, you'll turn the last page with the conviction that you, too, can and should lead change because, truly, there is no limit to the change that women can bring about. **So go forth and lead, #Firestarter.**

Sincerely,
A'shanti F. Gholar
Founder, The Brown Girls' Guide to Politics
Executive Director, Emerge

Introduction

"Each of us has a fire in our hearts for something. It's our goal in life to find it and keep it lit."

Mary Lou Retton

Since you've picked up this book, I know you feel it—an urge to make a difference, to create change, to use your unique gifts to bring a bold vision to life.

That urge might burn bright when you read a headline that angers you or when you see a need in your community. It might subside to a low flame when you're busy and distracted. But it's always there. Always reminding you of the mission that's calling you.

Friend, it's your time. The universe knows you are ready. It knows you have the desire, smarts, and most importantly, the passion. Your life has prepared you for this very moment.

What comes up for you when I say that? Thoughts like these?

Okay, but I don't even know where to start.

Where am I going to find the money to make this happen?

Yes, I have a lot of ideas, but I'm BUSY.

There are lots of paths I could take, but which one is the right one?

Is it even possible for someone like me to accomplish something like this?

I'm not good enough.

I wish I had a role model or a mentor.

That's where I come in. Like you, I've always heard that voice telling me to make the world a better place, that I am responsible for what's around me.

That voice has led me to some amazing experiences—from the newsroom to the campaign trail, from legislatures to a desert in the middle of the night.

I learned a lot along the way. And, more and more, it's been on my heart to share what I know. I dreamed of creating the kind of book that I had wished for early in my journey. A book with both inspiration and practical, no-nonsense advice. A book to awaken possibilities and to create community.

You're holding the results of my dream right now.

Meet the #Firestarters

In these pages, I will introduce you to some amazing women I call #Firestarters. What is a #Firestarter? It's someone who sees a need and who starts a movement that's bigger than herself to answer that need. A #Firestarter hustles hard. She brings people together. And she leaves a legacy.

Get ready to meet...

The Groundbreaker: Alejandrina Guzman
When she beat the odds to survive, her parents told her she was in this world for a reason. As a groundbreaking student leader, she discovered it.

The Trailblazer: Rina Shah
A veteran of the political scene, she works to make sure all voices are heard—on both sides of the aisle.

The Innovator: Monica Kang
After transforming her own life with creativity, she turned what she learned into a movement she's expanded internationally.

The Strategist: Lauren Harper
A state presidential campaign leader at twenty-five, she wants to give rising generations a place at the table.

The Inspirer: Jarinete Santos
An activist since middle school, today she's on a mission to show all women that they have the potential to lead.

The Gamer-Changer: Kishshana Palmer
She gets things *done*, from the world of fundraising to her current journey as an entrepreneur who empowers others.

The Candidate: Amanda K. Edwards
A champion for the future in Houston, she's now aiming to create meaningful change on a whole new level.

The Dreamer: Claudia Yoli Ferla
Young people can rewrite the story of this country, she believes. And her own American story is an amazing one.

The Founder: Ashley Cheng
Shaken by the 2016 election, this communications pro found a way to turn her activism into her full-time job.

The Survivor: Karen Hansen
By sharing her story, this designer gives a voice to the voiceless and takes a stand against victim-blaming.

The Elected: Tishaura Jones
She never thought she would follow her father's footsteps into politics. But when she did, she changed lives.

The Amplifier: Tatiana Torres
Her story is the American dream of opportunity—a dream she fights for others to be able to live too.

The Activist: Angela Provost
With farming in her blood, she works to protect and restore a vanishing agricultural heritage.

These #Firestarters will candidly share their stories: the highs and lows, the wins and losses, and everything in between. And they'll give you the same ideas, encouragement, advice, and tough love they would if you were sitting down with them over coffee or wine.

I guarantee you'll see yourself in their stories. And, as you do, you'll realize *you* can do big things, just like they have.

From Inspiration to Action

But becoming a #Firestarter yourself takes more than inspiration. You have to turn that inspiration into action. So after you read the #Firestarter stories, I want you to dive right into the tools section of this book to start bringing your movement to life. I'll teach you my Firestarter Formula, the same framework that I have used to launch movements that have impacted the lives of millions of people.

Here's a little preview:

The World Needs Your Spark

I have to be honest with you; I worry about how history is going to remember us. Will our descendants wonder why we were so complacent and regressive? Why we blindly trusted old systems? Why we didn't take our responsibilities more seriously?

The world needs #Firestarters. And we need you to join us—urgently.

As I type this, I'm watching as CNN airs graphic video of injured people lying outside a Walmart in El Paso after a mass shooting. People are screaming. Parents are trying to find their children.

Tears are running down my face. For El Paso. For Texas, the state where I live. The tears flow from my anger that horrific events like these keep happening. And they flow from my frustration that I can't fix everything overnight.

All those "thoughts and prayers" messages on social media won't change a thing when it comes to mass shootings. Or our broken health care system. Or the inequities that continue to plague our society.

You know what will, though? #Firestarters like you—running for office, raising money, starting social-minded businesses, lifting their voices.

None of this is easy. But we've got to do this, y'all. And do it together. That's why I wrote this book. So are you ready to spark change? Let's get started!

My #Firestarter Story

I told you a little about myself in the Introduction, but since we're doing the work of #Firestarters together, I thought you might want to get to know me a little better.

As far back as I can remember, I have wanted to make the world a better place. When I was a little girl in Lafayette, Louisiana, that meant I wanted to be a doctor. I also considered being the principal of the world's largest school. I remember leaning a chalkboard against a twin bed and then seating all my dolls around it. Hey, when you're born with community service in your DNA, it shows up in even your childhood games.

I come from a long line of change-makers with deep roots within the Catholic tradition. Both my father's and mother's parents volunteered at their churches. However, this was during the segregation era, so they likely didn't see the work as volunteerism. Instead, I'm sure it felt like "doing what we've got to do to keep the lights on."

When the community of Truman, Louisiana decided it wanted a church in its neighborhood, my mother's parents, Novella and Alton, stepped up to help guide the movement. They built a church they were proud of and one they could serve. I remember my grandmother helping at the church fair. She would carefully plan the menu to lower expenses and increase revenue for Our Lady Queen of Peace's bottom line. (Meanwhile, waistlines were expanding because of her crawfish etouffee and gumbo. I can still smell them!)

My parents, Pete and Carole, picked up the tradition. They helped found chapters of the Knights of St. Peter Claver and the Ladies Auxiliary, Courts #206. They were the Grand Knight and

Grand Lady (chapter leaders) at the same time. Our home was also a respite for traveling priests with my parents welcoming them in with a spirit of hospitality and kindness.

Opportunity After Defeat

I knew I wanted to follow my family's example of serving others, and by the time I was sixteen, I was clearer on how that might look for me. I wanted to share information with people that would allow them to make decisions about their lives. That "aha moment" came when I had the opportunity to be a teen reporter for KLFY-TV in my hometown and that framework still directs every career decision I make to this day.

I headed for college at Louisiana State University. (Geaux, Tigers!) I ran for student government—and lost, but then an opportunity came up to be appointed to a special counsel. I had a choice: Be proud and say "no," or take on the position even though I had been burned.

I came to a realization: The choice was bigger than me. I had an opportunity to be a role model and chip away at the stigma that African Americans didn't get involved on campus. So I said "yes" to leading by example—another ongoing theme in my life.

A New Direction

Even before graduating from college, I returned to television news for a while. As the youngest in the newsroom, I quickly learned to stand on my own two feet. I couldn't be afraid of those who had more experience or authority.

A quick stint as a fundraiser for a children's museum followed, and then a life-transforming opportunity came along. I worked for an amazing US Senate candidate doing communications and press for South Carolina's biggest election cycle. My candidate sought to replace Strom Thurmond after his retirement. It was a really big deal.

I never imagined a career in politics, but it made sense. After all, I was doing exactly what I set out to do: giving people information to make decisions about their lives and communities. And it was especially meaningful to do this for a leader who wanted to turn the election into a movement for good.

That movement came to an end, though, when our opponent won the election. This meant I was unemployed—without a plan for what was next.

But, on election night, a mentor provided some direction. The advice? Consider becoming a lobbyist.

The Unlikely Lobbyist

Just three months later, I was walking up the front steps of the Louisiana State Capitol.

Pause for a moment and picture this. This hike wasn't like five steps. It was *long*. But I marched up those stairs and straight to the information booth. I needed to know how to get a lobbyist badge—and where the bathroom was.

I was a most unlikely lobbyist. Before that day, the last time I had been in the Capitol was my fifth-grade field trip. I had no pedigree, no family connections, and no political action committee (PAC) checks to hand out.

What I *did* have was a passion for a cause and the ability to bring people together, and I was positive (or at least optimistic) that I could use those things to advocate for change.

My opponents were mostly male. There were maybe thirty female lobbyists in the building and fewer than a third of them were women of color.

Just as in the newsroom, I was "the kid." Seriously. I was the same age as many of my colleagues' children.

They all said the same things about me. "She's sweet." "She's so nice." I can't tell you how many times I wanted to add, "And she's about to kick your...."

There's Always, Always a Way

After Hurricane Katrina, many at the Louisiana State Capitol said it would be impossible to pass any non-hurricane legislation. At the time, I was working for the American Heart Association. My organization wanted me to pass a bill that would make all workplaces in the state smoke-free, including restaurants and bars.

While I knew that passing this bill would be tough, I didn't back down. I worked around the clock building a coalition, training spokespeople to speak to the press or at town halls, and communicating our plan for implementation.

It wasn't easy. Building movements never is, especially when coalitions are involved. I had to fight not only to keep the coalition together but also to push back on proposed amendments that didn't fit the spirit of the bill. The industry was working just as hard as I was—taking lawmakers to fancy dinners or on riverboat rides, handing out PAC checks.

I refused to give up. I adopted the motto, "There's always, always a way." I still tell myself this every day, and these words are even on a plaque hanging in my closet.

Finally, with faith, fortitude, and a lot of tears, I watched the Louisiana Smoke-Free Air Act of 2006 get signed into law. I was twenty-eight. It was one of the defining moments in my career.

Finding the Formula

Shortly thereafter, I became a vice president of government relations responsible for staff and contractors across a multi-state region.

It was during this time that I started thinking about how to teach others how to do what I had done with the Smoke-Free Air Act. I began to hone the Firestarter Formula, which I will teach you later in this book, to coach others.

I also began to build a platform to teach others everything I had learned. It has now grown to include a blog, videos, podcasting, speaking engagements, and this book.

Leaving a Legacy

Soon after I got engaged, the church my grandparents helped raise and where my parents walked down the aisle burned. My dream of getting married there was in ashes.

There was never a question of whether the church would be rebuilt. My father and Pastor Hampton Davis launched a capital campaign. They rallied others to raise the millions of dollars needed. I can still hear my father saying "The money to build the church is right here in this very church. It's in the pockets of you in the pews."

Just months after the church reopened its doors, we held the funeral for my father at the very altar he helped select. That church is his legacy. It's a part of him we still have even now that he's gone.

In the same way, this book is part of my legacy, and I hope it will spur you to think about your own.

Alejandrina Guzman
The Groundbreaker

"Who's in the room making decisions – and who's not? Who's been left out of the conversation?"

A #Firestarter's Beginnings

Sometimes it takes a #Firestarter a while to find her spark.

And then there's Alejandrina Guzman.

Alejandrina—the first Latina student body president at the University of Texas at Austin (UT) and the first differently abled student to serve in that role in the entire Big 12 Conference—is a born fighter.

Now, I know a lot of people *say* that. But in her case, it's quite literally true.

When Alejandrina was born, she wasn't breathing. Medical personnel filled the delivery room. Her parents—immigrants from Mexico—did not speak English, and only one nurse could speak Spanish and communicate with them.

After nine and a half long minutes, Alejandrina finally drew her first breath.

But her fight wasn't over.

Alejandrina was born with diastrophic dysplasia. This condition affects the bones and cartilage, causing short limbs and other developmental differences.

Doctors told her parents that Alejandrina, their first child, would not survive past twenty-four hours.

When she proved those dire predictions wrong, doctors kept cautioning her parents throughout her first year of life that the odds were against her.

Wrong again.

Her dramatic arrival shaped Alejandrina's life going forward. As she grew up in Azle, Texas—a small city near Fort Worth—her parents always told her she was in this world for a reason.

"My parents have always instilled in me a 'you *can* do it' attitude," she says.

If, for example, she told them she couldn't reach something, they would ask her "You can't—or you don't want to?"

With loving and empowering parents, she grew into a resourceful young woman. After high school graduation, she headed to UT as a first-generation college student.

Finding Her Fire

Given what Alejandrina went on to accomplish, you might be assuming that she arrived on campus with her sights set on being elected to student government, but that's not quite what happened.

Over her first couple of years on campus, she saw student government as elitist, unhelpful, and not attentive enough to underrepresented students. In fact, Alejandrina will freely tell you that she was probably the loudest complainer about student government in her friend group.

But then she found herself in a conversation that surprised her—and that changed everything.

Alejandrina was talking with a friend who mentioned that student government elections were coming up. She thought the friend was going to ask her to join a campaign.

But instead, her friend said she thought it was time for a change in student government, and she suggested that Alejandrina run.

"I started laughing out loud," Alejandrina says.

But the idea stayed with her. She consulted with other friends. She went back and forth with herself. Maybe she *could* create change?

Finally, with the deadline looming, she filed her paperwork to run for one of eight university-wide representative seats. There were eighteen other candidates.

"I ended up being first place," she says. "And I couldn't believe it!"

But student government wasn't the only way Alejandrina was shining ever brighter as a #Firestarter. She became involved at UT's Multicultural Engagement Center where she was surrounded by other people of color and felt a real sense of being at home.

"That really molded me into the leader and the activist that I am today," she says.

She also began to see some of her experiences growing up in a mostly white town in a different way—like when her mother told her kindergarten teacher Alejandrina's name and the teacher responded with "Oh, okay. So we're going to go with *Ali*."

"None of that hit me until I got to UT," she says.

Another big step in Alejandrina's development as a leader was working on the campaign for her friend, Jesse Guadiana, when he was seeking to become student government vice president. Through his campaign, Alejandrina gained experience dealing with issues like racism and xenophobia she would soon have to navigate herself.

But she also gained deeper insight into how meaningful it was to serve as well as a greater sense of her own potential. If Jesse saw her trying to multitask during a meeting, he would remind her "Pay attention. You're next."

And she was.

Jesse's ticket didn't win, and that was tough for Alejandrina, but seeing how student leaders had a place at the table when big decisions were made, she later decided to run for student body president herself.

Her story brings back a lot of memories for me. At LSU, I worked on a multicultural student government campaign ticket. Like Alejandrina, I experienced painful loss when my candidates weren't elected. But, also like her, I found a new opportunity because others saw my spark—serving as director of minority affairs for student government. In that role, I founded a group that helped create a pipeline of student government candidates of color.

With all of the "firsts" of Alejandrina's election, she made history and has had an untold impact just by being who she is. I can only imagine what it would have been like having a role model like her as I grew up with an "invisible disability" myself. After tumbling into a coffee table when I was learning to walk, I lost hearing in my left ear and sight in my left eye.

But her accomplishments didn't stop there.

One of the things Alejandrina is most proud of is establishing an initiative for first-generation college students. Her project connected them with resources and helped show them that they were not alone in what they were feeling. It also led to the creation of a scholarship for first-generation students to attend Camp Texas, an orientation for incoming UT students.

Creating something new was a lot of work. Alejandrina honed her ability to create buy-in by collaborating with administrators, different campus offices, and even alumni, but it was all more than worth it.

That inclusive approach became a defining quality of her administration. She and her executive team made a point of bringing other students from different segments to their meetings with administrators. They would invite students who were already doing work around the topic being discussed at a particular meeting—for example, mental health. It was important to her to use her access to administrators to give a voice to other students as well. She wouldn't speak first or speak the most because she wanted to create the space for other leaders to be heard. Alejandrina feels that these efforts ultimately recalibrated how both UT administrators and students think about working together.

Spreading Her Spark

Even though Alejandrina has already accomplished so much, she's still very much at the beginning of her journey as a #Firestarter. Today she does community outreach and fundraising for a local political campaign in Austin. She's also on the board for People United for Mobility Action in Austin.

"I've gotten to really dive deep in local politics," she says.

Serving as student government president at UT helped set her on the path she's on now.

"I would not trade it for the world," she says. "I'm beyond lucky, beyond privileged, beyond honored to have been in that position; at the same time acknowledging it was really, really hard!"

She came away with an understanding of systemic issues and of how to navigate bureaucracy.

"How do you make your voices heard? How do you protest in a way that's loud and powerful and bold? I learned *a lot* of those things," she says.

Her role as president also showed her what it truly means to be an ally.

"Who's in the room making decisions—and who's not?" she says. "Who's been left out of the conversation?"

In her current work, she's especially focused on outreach to the Latinx and disability communities to encourage voting and to help them be educated about and engaged in the political process.

So what does the future hold? Alejandrina could see herself working in a state or national campaign or perhaps using her relationship-building skills in work with the legislature.

Whatever she does, she believes strongly in "providing that platform for other people to rise up." In everything she does, "it's going to be all about empowering people."

That's what being a leader means to Alejandrina. "It's not me taking up the space," she says. "It's bringing people with me wherever I go."

Ignite Your Own Fire

What can you take away from Alejandrina's story to catalyze your own movement?

What's your story?

Alejandrina grew up hearing a powerful message from her parents: You're in this world for a reason. That helped her conquer a lot of challenges. Did your family instill in you your own story that can be a source of strength for you now? If not, it's time to rewrite your story to one that feels truer and more empowering.

Own who you are

Wherever you want to go in this life, the first step is to "own what you're good at," Alejandrina says. Remind yourself of all the stuff you've already made happen. This is a great thing to do particularly when you're experiencing imposter syndrome. We all go through feelings of self-doubt sometimes, but you can't let them douse your flame. The next time you feel like you don't know what you're doing, remember "that's okay because *no one* knows what they're doing," Alejandrina says with her ever-present laugh.

Pay attention

Alejandrina could have just shrugged off her friend's suggestion that she run for student government. Remember, it seemed improbable to her at the time. But something about the idea stuck with her, and she paid attention to that. Do you have a thought that you can't shake? What might it be trying to tell you?

Embrace failure

Do you have anxieties about failure? Alejandrina reminds you that anytime you're doing big things and challenging yourself, it's not a matter of *if* you're going to mess up. It's more a question of *when* it's going to happen. And when it does happen, remember that you're not alone. Every single #Firestarter before you has experienced setbacks, mistakes, and just plain goof-ups. "Everyone talks about success, but no one really talks about the failures," Alejandrina says. The important question *isn't* how you're going to avoid failure. Instead, it's how to become a person who's really good at bouncing back.

Bring other people along

One of the many things I love about Alejandrina's story is that she *isn't* about power for its own sake. She's always thinking of ways to help others get their voices heard too. What might this look like in your own movement? How can you give others a platform?

Make the most of mentors

The importance of mentorship is a theme that surfaced again and again in my interviews with #Firestarters, and Alejandrina is no different. For Alejandrina, an important mentor was her friend Jesse who both encouraged her potential and gave her concrete experience she used in her campaign for UT student body president. #Firestarter, if you don't currently have the right mentors in your life, just imagine me and Alejandrina giving you a little nudge and saying "You're next" just as Jesse did for her because we firmly believe that it's true!

Rina Shah
The Social Trailblazer

"Don't think twice. You're ready to serve."

A Firestarter's Beginnings

Last year, a good friend said "Terri, if you want to meet the ultimate #Firestarter, you need to meet Rina Shah." When I finally had a chance to sit down with Rina, I realized that my friend could not have been more right.

Rina is a Republican political adviser, media contributor, and social entrepreneur as well as an ardent advocate for getting more women to run for political office.

In a word, Rina Shah is a trailblazer.

Her father was raised in Uganda where, going back for generations, the family worked as merchants. When the dictator Idi Amin came to power, he declared genocide on non-black Ugandans. The family had deep roots in Uganda, but overnight, Rina's grandparents and seven of her dad's sisters were forced to flee the country and resettle in the United Kingdom.

At the time they fled, Rina's father was in India attending medical school. While living in India, he met Rina's mother who was working as a lawyer. They immigrated to the US ten years apart.

Growing up in southern West Virginia in a multi-generational household, Rina learned about the persecution faced by her father's family. These stories had a profound impact on Rina. "For me, there was a sense that yes, any government can get too big and powerful," she says. "Government can get too oppressive, and we really shouldn't fully trust it."

Rina says that her family didn't lean left or right, Democrat or Republican, blue or red. "My parents were more purple than anything else," she explains. "They always believed that being civically involved was something that we all should do because of the country we've been given where we're able to voice our desires, hopes, opinions, views, all of that without any fear of retaliation or fatal consequences."

Finding Her Fire

When she was about age seven or eight, Rina obsessively carried around a book called *What Do You Know About the American Presidents?* She read and reread it. Little did she know that one day she'd work as a top strategist, spokesperson, and head of communications for two US presidential candidates.

But it wasn't a straight path from her childhood passion to a political career. In fact, it's only now that Rina looks back and sees her zeal for that dog-eared book as a sign of what her future would hold. In fact, in 2002, Rina entered the honors program at West Virginia University on an engineering scholarship. She thought her life's passion was technology and wasn't even considering a career in politics.

So what happened?

During her freshman year in college, Rina was looking to make some extra money, so she answered an ad in the campus daily newspaper. The ad was placed by another college newspaper that called itself "the alternative to the campus daily." The position advertised was for a copy editor. Rina really had no idea what "the alternative to the campus daily" meant, but she loved writing and editing and figured she could do the job.

She got the job—one that would wind up changing the trajectory of Rina's career. As she corrected reporters' grammar, she slowly realized that this was the conservative student newspaper, and it was indirectly funded by the renowned conservative think tank, The Heritage Foundation. The mainstream daily newspaper as actually considered liberal, at least by those at the outlet where Rina worked.

By Rina's senior year, she worked as the managing editor, and The Heritage Foundation flew her to Washington, DC where she attended talks by conservative political theorists and was given a bookcase full of political titles.

She learned The Heritage Foundation was devoted to promoting conservative principles and policies that supported free enterprise, limited government, individual freedom, traditional American values, and a strong national defense.

"I quickly realized that these were my views," Rina says. "I found that I believed a lot of what I was reading and became more passionate about taking those messages into our society."

Once Rina graduated college, she got a job as a reporter for a local CBS affiliate news station. Many stories she covered took her to impoverished areas of West Virginia where she found residents hoping and praying for the government to solve their problems. Rina felt profoundly sad to meet so many people who seemed to be waiting endlessly for government help—assistance that would seldom arrive, and if it did, then it would be too little too late.

But this sadness Rina felt also lit her fire.

She quit her job at the television station, packed her bags, and moved to Washington, DC with the intention of figuring out how to best help people living in poverty in West Virginia.

For her first few years in Washington, Rina completed several paid internships. She also worked as a fitness instructor and a tutor for elementary and middle school students. In the process, she learned her way around the city. During this time, she worked toward attending law school so that she could affect change through the criminal justice system, but then a friend recommended her for an entry-level staff assistant job for a New Jersey congressman. Rina figured it wouldn't hurt to interview.

Not only did she get hired, but she was hired for a much higher-level role than she'd interviewed for and became the congressman's right-hand woman. "This all happened really quickly, but when they offered me the job, I didn't think twice and accepted it. Suddenly, I had a direction and what seemed like a lifelong career. Suddenly, I was part of something that was much bigger than me and where I grew up," she explains.

From there, this #Firestarter really started a blaze.

Spreading Her Spark

Rina went on to make a name for herself on Capitol Hill. In 2010, she moved to another congressman's office, working as his senior staffer for over a year.

Soon, she caught the campaign bug and left Capitol Hill to join a longshot bid for the White House. Longtime, California-based political activist and actor Fred Karger asked her to join his inner circle. In 2012, Karger became the first-ever openly gay presidential candidate from a major party, and he ran as a Republican.

In 2016, she became chief spokesperson and one of the top strategists for Evan McMullin who ran as an Independent and as the Republican Party alternative to Donald Trump. "Looking back on it now, I have to pinch myself because here was a young girl who was obsessed with the American Presidency but from a small town with no ties to anyone big, famous, or rich in law or politics. Yet I was able to serve in the senior leadership on two US presidential campaigns. I'm living the American dream," she says.

Through her work, Rina developed expertise in speech-writing and building winning strategies for political campaigns at all levels of government. As a public affairs and government consultant, she has advised a wide range of domestic and international corporations, including startup ventures, and she has served on many nonprofit boards.

Rina is determined to use her skills to make the political landscape more equitable, particularly for women and those with a minority voice. To realize her mission, she co-founded the Women's Public Leadership Network, which provides women with the knowledge and resources to make running for elected office and engaging in the political process more accessible.

"We have a dearth of women at all levels of elected office across the country, and we women make up more than half the population," Rina explains. "I'm not saying we need quotas so we make up half of everything, but we need to be better represented. Until we're better represented, we're not going to get the laws and policies that reflect us and would better serve us and our families."

Rina also serves on the advisory boards of several other organizations including RepresentWomen, which aims to elect more women to government, and VoteRunLead, the largest candidate training program for women.

No matter where you are on the political spectrum, if you're a woman with a heart for public service, Rina encourages you to get involved in politics. "Never doubt that you have what it takes to be an incredible public servant," she says. "If you've ever had the itch—a sense to say 'serving my country in this way looks interesting to me'—I would say do it. Go all in. That's what men do. They don't think twice and second guess themselves. You're ready to serve."

As a person of color, Rina is also committed to recruiting more minorities to serve. She co-founded Catalyst Political Action Committee, which aims to diversify the GOP by recruiting and supporting candidates from a variety of racial, ethnic, religious, and sexual orientation back-grounds.

She recommends first attending a political party meeting to see if you feel a connection with that group of people, and then consider joining a political club. And, she says, it's important to make your intentions known: Tell people that you want to be a political appointee or run for office. She says that you will find people who will open doors for you and show you how to get to where you want to be.

Also, of course, Rina urges you to contact any of the organizations which she has served, past or present. Send a message through the organization's website and someone will get back to you and ask "What do you want to do? How do you want to get involved? What's on your mind?" Spend some time in advance thinking carefully about how you will reply.

One other way that Rina spreads her spark is by providing political analysis and commentary on national television. She regularly appears on Al Jazeera Media Network, MSNBC and the PBS show, *To the Contrary*. I was curious what it's like for her to appear on a Democratic-leaning cable network since it seems like television hosts are always looking to get panelists to fight and say something sensationalist.

"I've always been a collaborative spirit, even more so now that I'm the mother of a toddler and a preschooler," she explains. "When I'm on these panels, I'm not looking for a fight. I'm looking to hear the other person. I go on and speak my truth, and treat it like a conversation between two people who have different life experiences and see things a different way. We're taught that in school to respectfully disagree, but that's what's missing in today's media landscape. There's not much civility. I try to bring that civility."

Ignite Your Own Fire

What can you take away from Rina's story to catalyze your own movement?

Search your roots

When Rina was unsure of her path forward, her family story and childhood passions seemed to point the way. If you're looking for what will light your fire, think back to your roots. Is there something in your family history that resonates with you or that could give you direction?

For Rina, hearing how her father's family had to flee Uganda made her a true believer in the principles of limited government. And now, in retrospect, she realizes that carrying around the book about American presidents could have provided a clue to what she truly loves.

Proclaim your intention

Once you figure out what's most important to you and the direction you want to go, join groups of like-minded people. This may be a political party or an advocacy group. Then find mentors and announce what you'd like to achieve. Rina used this strategy repeatedly as she worked her way up and around Capitol Hill. When you speak your objective aloud, other people can help you get to where you want to go.

Make the leap

When Rina got the job offer to work for the congressman from New Jersey, she went with her gut and took the position even though it seemed to come out of the blue and derail her plan to attend law school. Sometimes something just feels right, and you've got to jump in with both feet. Rina especially advises women who might want to run for office to make the leap and don't overthink it.

Blaze a new trail

Rina is a woman of color in today's Republican Party. She believes in freedom for same-sex couples to marry or to at least have civil unions. She also says that while she is pro-life for herself, she believes every woman has the right to decide what to do with her own body.

In all these ways, Rina represents a minority position within the Republican Party. But this doesn't make her want to leave the party—it makes her want to work toward positive change from within. That's why she's started so many trailblazing organizations while remaining affiliated with the Republican Party.

If you don't see the advocacy or political organization that represents your point of view, consider starting one that does. You're likely to find others who feel overjoyed to finally have a place where they belong.

Talk to people who are different from you

If you want to be a changemaker, reach across the aisle and talk to people with different points of view. Just by having a respectful conversation with someone who has opposing views, you will be making a difference and taking a stand for civility. This is what Rina tries to do when she appears on television panels, and this is what you can do in your community.

Monica Kang
The Social Entrepreneur

*"You have to always stay open-minded and
thoughtful and be a creative problem solver."*

A #Firestarter's Beginnings

Monica Kang may have never anticipated that she would make an impact in the world by teaching creativity, but she always knew that she wanted to make a mark somehow.

She grew up in a family that set the stage for her to become a #Firestarter. They valued female leadership and encouraged her to speak her mind. As she did, her family helped her sharpen her ideas and the way she expressed them by giving her feedback and asking questions. This instilled a deep curiosity in Monica. Even today, friends will tell her that she asks a lot of questions. Sounds like a #Firestarter, right?

Her love of reading also came from her family. Reading about great leaders got her wondering about what she could accomplish herself someday and what her unique contribution to the world could be.

Monica was also influenced by experiencing different cultures. Born in Washington, DC, she spent her elementary and middle school years in South Korea. While her parents stayed in South Korea, she returned to the US for high school and college, and work experiences have taken her to Europe and Asia. She's been everywhere!

"Humility and filial piety are a key part of Asian culture, and I'm grateful that I grew up with that," she explains. "It helps me think about things not just from my point of view but from a collaborative point of view."

Her upbringing helped her understand that we are all just people, and we all have strengths and weaknesses. It also made her more mindful.

"I think it's so fascinating to know how we're all connected and impact one another in different ways," Monica says.

Growing up in different cultures also gave Monica an interest in diplomacy and international affairs, which helped guide her toward work in nuclear nonproliferation early in her career. The work intrigued her because of the importance of communication and collaboration. She was doing something she loved and was passionate about, but then something changed.

Finding Her Fire

Because Monica cared so much about her job, she was perplexed when she started feeling stuck and depressed. It wasn't that she lacked a sense of purpose. After all, "preventing nuclear weapons from going to the bad guys" is a *pretty clear* purpose.

To address her depression, Monica started with small steps—like walking instead of taking the bus—and noticing how those changes affected her. Walking, for example, got her out in fresh air, kept her off her phone, and made her more observant of the world around her. All of those small decisions started building on each other and leading Monica to new mental shifts. She went from feeling stuck to loving her job and excelling at it. Clients sought her out because she would help them think in different ways.

People could tell that Monica had made a transformation, and they wanted to know how she did it; so Monica began to realize that she might be the right person to "connect the dots" for others on how to cultivate their own creativity. She saw that too many people still felt that creativity wasn't something for them, which made her feel there had to be better, more accessible ways to teach it. Opening creativity up to more people was important to Monica because we don't just need creativity at work. We need it to be healthy, thriving humans. When we're creative, we just bring a whole different energy to every interaction.

That's what led Monica to launch InnovatorsBox in 2016. Through the company, she has taught creativity to Fortune 500 companies, nonprofits, and higher education institutions. Facebook, Ericsson, and Citibank are just a few of InnovatorsBox's clients. Monica also speaks at conferences and for organizations.

"We think about culture and leadership and team development and what that creative inclusivity means," Monica says. "I do a lot of interactive sessions and programming to help them rethink about that in a fun and practical way."

But Monica knew that she couldn't reach everyone she wanted to just through speaking, so she wrote a book, *Rethink Creativity: How to Innovate, Inspire, and Thrive at Work*. InnovatorsBox also offers tools you can use on your own with a team. Infinity Cards, for example, push you to ask deeper questions to find better solutions.

The feedback Monica gets on her work lets her know her movement is on the right track. People who didn't think they were creative start realizing they are—and getting excited about what they can create. She also hears from people who tell her that she has given them courage to share their ideas and to try their things their company has never done before because they've been scared. Making these breakthroughs, of course, takes great vulnerability and empathy.

All of that affects her deeply, Monica says. "I'm also Christian, so I think a lot about faith in the whole equation of the role I'm playing," she says. Her work "gives me a humbling opportunity to connect with a lot of different stakeholders that I never thought I could." Sometimes that looks like a veteran manager having a heart-to-heart conversation with her about how she helped them change. And sometimes it looks like a teenager who says that seeing her gives them the confidence they can be a leader one day too.

She understands that her presence itself can send a powerful message. Monica says there aren't many Asians *or* Millennials on the speaking platform at some of the events to which she's invited.

A person who saw her speaking gave her a compliment she remembers: "I can feel that you're Korean with your humility, but I can feel that you're American with your confidence."

"That meant a lot because it really made me think about how I can relate to those two different communities," Monica says. "I'm able to honor both values, which took a long time to appreciate and tie together."

Spreading Her Spark

Monica wants to see the movement she started with InnovatorsBox spread even further.

"I would like to figure out how do we do a more cost-effective, scalable global movement where we reach the right audience," she says. That's a challenge for a small company with a small marketing budget.

She also wants InnovatorsBox to spur some lasting changes in how we all think about work and creativity. What if we…

…stopped treating people like their job titles define them?

…saw the wisdom that someone could bring who has transitioned from another career field?

…treated having multiple passions as a positive?

…put culture and creativity at the heart of everything?

"I'm only at the tip of the iceberg, just learning how I can help more people and in the right way and in the most effective way," Monica says.

Ignite Your Own Fire

What can you take away from Monica's story to catalyze your own movement?

Tap into your heritage

The values that Monica grew up with—empathy, connection, humility, and collaboration—shape her work today. What aspects of your own background define who you are and could be assets to your movement?

Follow your North Star

No matter what the movement is that you want to start, you need what Monica calls a "clear North Star:" a well-defined goal or destination. You also must have the self-knowledge to understand how your strengths and weaknesses will affect both how you reach that North Star and what will keep you going during the journey.

Stay flexible

The map to your North Star will be ever-changing. "You're going to quickly realize there's no one way to get there," Monica says. Very often, what seems like the right way initially isn't the best option after all. "You have to always stay open-minded and thoughtful, and be a creative problem solver through the process." While unknowns can be scary, they can also be exhilarating. Maybe the path will be different than you thought it was going to be, but your impact also ends up being greater than you ever imagined.

Use the tough stuff

Monica isn't immune to challenges like anxiety, impostor syndrome, or scarcity mindset when it comes to her own creativity. But she sees the value in difficult moments because they help her better understand what her clients and audiences are feeling and how to better help them. What could your own challenges be trying to teach you?

Be business savvy

If, like Monica, your movement involves starting a business, remember that the key word here is "business." Do you have a revenue model? Do you know who your buyer is? "If not, it's a hobby," Monica says. She gets it: You want to start making a difference *now*, but you still must take the time to think through the execution of your business. If you don't, you set yourself up for discouragement, and you limit your long-term impact.

Assemble your support squad

A movement is never a single person. "Keep surrounding yourself with as many allies as possible," Monica says. The right mentors, colleagues, and partners—who can support you strategically *and* emotionally—make all the difference. One of her own mentors gave her this formula: You need people who look like you and think like you, who don't look like you but who think like you, who look you but don't think like you, and who don't look like you or think like you. If there's no diversity in the people around you, you risk becoming narrow-minded, and that's not good for your movement.

Keep growing

Consistently devote time and energy to your own self-development, Monica recommends. "If leaders are not focusing on growing themselves, especially as a #Firestarter, then how do you envision walking the talk?" she says. If you're not cultivating your own creativity, for example, then how can you expect your team to grow its creativity? One thing Monica loves about her work is that she also benefits from all that she learns.

Refill your energy

Sure, you *could* push through and work a couple more hours tonight but using that time to get some extra sleep, spend time with loved ones, or otherwise take care of yourself might actually be more productive in the long run. "Sometimes you just need a break," Monica says. "So I've been more forgiving to myself if I need to slack off a little bit." After all, if you're mentally and physically fried, you will run out of the creativity and problem-solving capability you need to keep your movement going. So don't burn out, #Firestarter. We need you!

Lauren Harper
The Strategist

"If you expect this country to get any better, then you're going to have to include younger people in the conversation."

A #Firestarter's Beginnings

You're never too young or too old to be a #Firestarter, and Lauren Harper is proof of that. At twenty-five, she was the South Carolina state director for Democratic presidential candidate Beto O'Rourke. Running a statewide campaign organization isn't where she expected to be just a few years out of college, but when the opportunity appeared, she was ready to seize it.

It's no surprise that Lauren grew up in "a family of people who love people." The spirit of serving others is definitely in her DNA. Her grandfather (who passed away before she was born) was a union organizer in Buffalo, New York, and her mom and her aunt are active volunteers.

After graduating from South Carolina's Fort Mill High School, Lauren went on to the University of South Carolina where her love of writing inspired her to major in public relations. Through various internships with Columbia Mayor Steve Benjamin's office, a state representative, and a public affairs firm, she discovered that political work was a natural fit for her and a meaningful way to use her communication skills. "You look like you're in the right place," others would tell her.

She felt like she was in the right place too. So, after graduation, Lauren stepped into a full-time role as a communications and policy advisor for Mayor Benjamin.

"I spent the first year working for the mayor, trying to convince people I wasn't the intern," she says with a laugh. "So you're trying to gain respect and recognition. By the time you gain respect, you're like, 'Okay, *now* I can get stuff done because people actually take my thoughts and ideas as valid.'"

And Lauren *really* got stuff done. One of the accomplishments she's most proud of is starting a committee to help the city be more intentional in tackling food insecurity. She also worked on revamping the city's youth commission to get young people more interested in government.

All in all, Lauren was "happy as a clam" in the mayor's office, doing work she loved and knowing that she was making a difference for others.

She had no idea her life was about to change in a major way.

Finding Her Fire

"Out of the blue" Lauren got a call from Tyler Jones, a senior advisor for O'Rourke who knew Lauren and her strong track record. She told the campaign she needed some time to think about whether to join up. It was meeting the candidate himself that helped persuade her.

"It's very refreshing to see a candidate who's not just a genuine person but is thoughtful and inquisitive," she says.

Those descriptions apply to Lauren too. A big part of her job was building relationships throughout South Carolina. That meant showing up at events throughout the state to talk about O'Rourke, listening to residents' concerns, and assuring them that her candidate cares about them. That last part was especially important, she says, since South Carolinians often feel forgotten on the national political scene.

"People don't want a president who's going to make a lot of promises on the campaign trail and then not keep their word," she says.

In pop culture, campaign operatives are often portrayed as ruthless and conniving (think the television show *Veep*). But Lauren says that a very different approach is actually what gets results.

"Kindness goes so far," she says. "We're not talking about faking kindness as a means to manipulate others. People can spot that a mile off," Lauren says.

But, she adds, "when people recognize that you try to do good work and you try to do good by people, they take notice of it."

Spreading Her Spark

I talked with Lauren in the summer of 2019. In "political time," that's an eternity ago, especially considering how tumultuous s this election cycle, and a lot has happened since then, including the horrific August mass shooting in El Paso, O'Rourke's hometown. The candidate made headlines for his outspoken remarks on guns and the rhetoric from President Trump that O'Rourke felt was encouraging such violence. But in early November, with funds running low, O'Rourke decided to end his campaign. In announcing his withdrawal from the race, he urged his supporters to "continue our commitment to the country in whatever capacity we can."

Well, I can tell you this: Lauren will be bringing her energy and empathy to powerful movements for a long time to come. I can already see signs of her bright future. She has her own consulting firm, and she's pursuing a master's degree in public administration and policy (she took a leave of absence during the campaign). And, as this book headed to press, she had just accepted a new role as South Carolina co-chair of The Welcome Party, an organization encouraging independent voters to participate in the 2020 presidential primaries. She's definitely a #Firestarter— someone who sees a need that others ignore and works to get it done.

"I really care about the future of this country," she says. "And I know that there are a lot of people who don't have the opportunity to be in a place of influence. So whenever I am in a place of influence, I try to do good work so that other people can be helped by that influence."

She believes strongly that the opportunity to work in the public sector is a privilege. And, as she did with the Columbia mayor's office, she's still working to get young people interested in public service. Lauren even started the Heart of a Servant Scholarship, a $1,000 award for students at her alma mater, Fort Mill High School, who want to go into public service. "We've got to encourage and incentivize people to do this kind of work." (And, I'll add, *hard*, hard work.)

Mentors were a powerful impact on her own life, and now she's paying that forward.

"I have a lot of mentees," she says. "I'll tell them 'Look, I have a lot going on. But if you just want to come sit in my office with me and talk, we can do that…. I'm here for you.'"

Faith is another powerful factor that will continue to shape Lauren's path.

"I desire to live out the full life that God has for me, and I desire to just bring glory to His name because He's been really good to me," she says. "And so I hope that through the work I'm able to do for other people, I will be able to show people that you can be confident in who you are and you can also desire better for others…. You can do really cool stuff if you remain true to who you are and don't try to be someone you're not."

At the end of the day, it all comes down to this for her: "Try to do good work. Love people well. And don't forget why you started."

Ignite Your Own Fire

What can you take away from Lauren's story to catalyze your own movement?

Be a mentor

No matter your age, you have experiences and wisdom from which younger people can learn, so how can you share it? How can you give them the same opportunities you had? If retirement is on the horizon for you, pass along your knowledge to ensure that someone else can keep doing the work that's important to you, Lauren says.

Bridge generations

"If you expect this country to get any better, then you're going to have to include younger people in the conversation," Lauren says. "You have to include them and their perspectives because they come from a totally different perspective than you." Even as someone who's on the younger end of the Millennial spectrum, she makes a point to listen to and learn from members of Generation Z.

Guide young #Firestarters

And speaking of Generation Z, if you're a Millennial or older, you can do so much to help these new #Firestarters. "What I'm noticing as I spend more time with younger people is they're just so passionate," Lauren says. "We have to be intentional about how we help them funnel that passion." For example, if they're angry about a political issue or even a controversy at school, help them find a way to protest or voice their opinion in a way that isn't going to come back and haunt them (like tweets that don't age well).

Pay attention

Even if you don't choose to work in politics as Lauren does, never forget that politics directly affects your life, and you have some responsibility to be involved. "Your local elections are very impactful," Lauren says. "So pay attention to who's on your city council, who your mayor is—and county council, legislators, governors—because those folks can really make or break a good life for you."

Remember your impact

All of the issues facing us can feel overwhelming sometimes, but you really can make a difference. Besides voting in or even running for office in local elections, consider getting involved in local boards, commissions, committees, and nonprofits, Lauren says. Engage more with your neighborhood, your church, or your kids' schools. The best way to channel your anxiety is to "look for the areas where you can touch someone's life in a more meaningful way," she says.

Light the way

If you need an extra push to stand out and to stand up for the things that are important to you, remember that other women are looking at your life to show them what's possible in their own. "You never know who's watching," Lauren says, recalling a friend in college who always seemed to be attending events and speaking. "I wanted to be like her. The visual is important; representation is important." No matter our age, other women's achievements can inspire us by showing possibilities for our own lives.

6

Jarinete Santos
The Inspirer

"My passion has driven me my whole life."

A #Firestarter's Beginnings

Sometimes our childhood and young adult experiences set the path our lives will follow. That's definitely true for Jarinete Santos. Today, Jarinete is the political pipeline director for She Should Run, an organization that aims to get more women running for office. But she was working for change well before that.

"There was a group in my middle school called Peace Jam, and essentially it was just like all the social justice nerds who didn't know that's what we were yet," she says.

The Peace Jam members did projects like painting over graffiti and cleaning up parks. Jarinete says it was also exciting to go to conferences with the cool older kids from the organization—high school students and even college freshmen.

"They were teaching us the importance of building community and of speaking up," she says. And Jarinete embraced the message wholeheartedly.

"I was *hooked*," she says. She loved feeling that she could make a difference for her community.

Her family was also very involved in their church, which gave a young Jarinete even more opportunities to serve and to experience leadership. As she did, Jarinete realized an essential truth about herself: "I like feeling empowered, and I like sharing that with others."

That's a theme that continued into her college years at Brigham Young University-Idaho. She quickly sought out service opportunities and became part of a student board for volunteer training. This helped her get even clearer on what she really loved doing. She began to understand that her passion was "investing in the volunteers themselves. I want them to feel good about themselves. I want them to have the right training to be successful because there's nothing worse than being a volunteer and feeling like you're failing."

After graduation, the political science major moved to Washington, DC, but she couldn't quite find her career groove.

Finding Her Fire

Then a tip from a friend helped Jarinete discover her true path. This friend taught leadership development courses for federal employees through an organization called the Partnership for Public Service, and she thought the kind of work she was doing might be a good match for Jarinete too.

It turns out that was an understatement.

"I was like, 'Wait, what? You get paid real money to talk to people—and it's public servants that you're talking to? Are you kidding me?... Oh my gosh, I could do this for a job. This is life-changing!'"

And her life really did change. She spent the next several years working with the Partnership for Public Service doing leadership development.

"I loved it so much," she says. It meant a lot to her to help people who had dedicated their lives to public service with the federal government.

Jarinete devoted herself to that role for several years before moving on to new opportunities with She Should Run in early 2019.

She was excited by the chance to help women feel empowered to run for office. She especially wanted to be an advocate for women of color, both in terms of developing them as candidates and in showing through her own presence that women of color should have a place at the table in conversations about leadership development. But she also points out that her job is advocating for *all* women, even those whose political beliefs differ from her own.

"It's really opened my eyes to what being committed to representation at large looks like," she says. "It's been really lovely as I've worked in this job to become more aware of the need for women that I might disagree with to have a place at the table as well."

She Should Run started out by enabling women to explore their interest in politics or civic engagement through self-navigated online training.

"They can learn about what it looks like to build their personal leadership style," Jarinete says, as well as tell their story, navigate social media, raise money, and even deal with sexism.

From there, She Should Run expanded to virtual and in-person cohorts where women are taught a curriculum via ninety-minute sessions once a week for seven weeks. Part of Jarinete's job is hiring the facilitators for those sessions.

"It's an inherently challenging audience because we're talking to the woman who has maybe never thought about running," she says. These are women who use the word "just" in describing themselves: I'm just a mom. I'm just a teacher. I'm just twenty-two. Reaching them isn't easy, but when they do have those "aha moments" about what they can do, it's incredibly satisfying, Jarinete says.

Besides working with the women served by She Should Run, Jarinete also values the chance she has to be a mentor to young women within the organization itself. By cultivating other #Firestarters, she has more impact than she ever could on her own.

Spreading Her Spark

Everything Jarinete has accomplished at She Should Run is particularly impressive when you consider that when she first saw the listing for her current job, she thought there was no way she could do it. (There's a lesson there, #Firestarters.)

"I have been more satisfied and surprised by my own capabilities in this job than I have in anything I've done previously," she says. There's just nothing like knowing that your combination of education, experience, and passion is helping build the future you want to see.

So what's Jarinete's vision for the future? Picture some high school students in their American government class. They are talking just as much about women who have led as men. "Women in leadership" isn't some special theme week in this class. It's part of what they learn every day because, in this future, women are equally represented in leadership. A woman leader isn't unusual or noteworthy. She's the norm.

Ignite Your Own Fire

What can you take away from Jarinete's story to catalyze your own movement?

Maybe *you* should run

Of course, Jarinete's number one tip for #Firestarters who have an interest in politics is checking out organizations like She Should Run. Remember, you don't need to have some detailed ten-year plan ("And then in 2028, I'll run for president...") to get involved with She Should Run. It's designed *exactly* for women who are just starting to explore their options. Visit sheshouldrun.org to learn more and find out whether She Should Run has any upcoming events planned for your area. I spoke at the organization's Road to Run: Austin event in 2019, and it was super-inspiring. What I love about their mission is that they prepare women to be community leaders and elected officials.

And if She Should Run is not your cup of tea, then there are plenty of other organizations from which to choose that include Emerge America, Vote Run Lead, Start Running, Women Campaign, and She The People. Some of these organizations lean toward one political ideology, but several are nonpartisan. I also recommend *The Brown Girls Guide to Politics* (www.thebgguide.com) for those who are not ready to receive training but who just want to listen to awe-inspiring women in politics!

Think locally

And as you do check out your options, Jarinete reminds you that holding local political office is an *awesome* way to start a movement. You don't have to turn your whole life upside down. "There are elected positions you can do on the side of your full-time job," she says.

Help some future #Firestarters

One thing that I love about Jarinete's story is the influence of the experiences she had through her church and through Peace Jam. If you also had some grown-ups nurturing you as a future #Firestarter, how can you pay that forward? And if you didn't, think about how powerful it would be to make sure things are different for the young girls who are in your life or in your community now.

Be a "yes" woman for yourself

However you decide to build your own movement, there'll be challenges to overcome. So don't create another challenge for yourself by standing in your own way, Jarinete says. She lives by some advice her mom once gave her: Always tell yourself "yes." Don't talk yourself out of going after that scholarship, job, fellowship, elected office, or whatever because you're scared you might not get it. Of course, you might end up hearing a "no" eventually, but you learn so much through the feedback and the experience. And, of course, you're going to hear "yes" plenty of times along the way too.

Step out and be seen

Here's another reason to just go for it when it comes to your goals: You'll be doing your part to create the world that Jarinete envisions—one where it's the norm for women to hold positions of power and leadership. Very often, the way that a woman realizes that something is possible for *her* to accomplish is that she sees another woman accomplishing it. So claim your opportunities to show other women what can be done, Jarinete urges. Run for office, seek a promotion, and tell your story. If the idea of being in the spotlight feels uncomfortable, remember that other women need to see you there.

Know that support is out there

So let's talk more about that discomfort. Does even the thought of telling others about your aspirations fill your head with visions of people making fun of you? Jarinete wants you to know others will probably be a lot more supportive than you're imagining. Instead of scoffing at your dreams, it's more likely they'll cheer you on.

Keep the door open

"If you're a woman who's made it, don't then close the door behind you and stop other women from making it," Jarinete says. Many of us grew up with the idea that there are only a finite number of women who can succeed and that we'd better fight pretty hard to be one of the few who do. That scarcity mentality hurts all of us. Jarinete encourages you to embrace the idea of abundance. "There is no limit to how far we can go as individuals and as a group," she says. "There's no reason for us to knock others down in our pursuit of that greatness." I often say, "If there's not room for you at the table, bring your own folding chair!"

Disagree the right way

Supporting other women does *not* mean never disagreeing with them. "I actually think we can reach better outcomes if we can disagree with one another," Jarinete says. One of the (many!) reasons we need more women leaders is so that women, like men, feel more comfortable hashing out their differences to reach the best solutions. But the key thing to remember is that disagreeing on the substance of someone else's remarks is constructive while criticizing another woman for something like her appearance or the way she talks most definitely isn't.

Own your passion

Has anyone ever told you that you're a bit, well, *much*? Don't let this silence you. "My passion has driven me my whole life," Jarinete says. "It is the number one factor I would credit for any success I've had." But her passion has sometimes been misinterpreted. She's even heard the S-word applied to her: shrill. "It has been frustrating because people will interpret my engagement as too high of emotion," she says. "I think this is something women face a lot." Don't get her wrong—she understands the importance of a professional demeanor. But you can be angry and still professional or enthusiastic and still professional. As she had to tell a former manager once, "Just because I show up differently doesn't mean I'm bad."

Kishshana Palmer
The Gamer-Changer

"I know how to galvanize people. I know how to marshal resources. I just know how to get stuff done."

A #Firestarter's Beginnings

When Kishshana Palmer was growing up in New York City, her friends decided they had the perfect nickname for her: Cash.

Why? Well, Kishshana was the go-to person any time there was a fundraiser—like a candy sale at school—going on.

"I was always coming up with some hairbrained scheme to raise money for whatever we needed to do," she says with a laugh.

Kishshana understood that the nickname stemmed from her friends' recognition of something special within her.

"I know how to galvanize people," she says. "I know how to marshal resources. I just know how to get stuff done."

It turns out her friends were on to something: Kishshana went on to a career in nonprofit leadership and then translated what she learned into her own consulting firm, Kishshana & Co.

So was she one of those people who figured out their mission in life early and then just got on the expressway to achieve their goals? Kishshana will quickly tell you that's not the case, but the journey she did take made her the #Firestarter she is today.

Like many of us, Kishshana lost touch with that early clarity she had about herself. High school felt like trying to figure out everything all over again.

Her mother and father, who came to the US from Jamaica, were profound influences on her.

"My parents really had a philosophy of work hard…"

She pauses for a beat, and I assume she's going to say "play hard."

"…*work hard*," she finishes. "They had a lot of influence over the way I saw myself and how I showed up in the world."

The oldest of four siblings, she was the first in her family to go to college. "There's a lot of pressure that comes with that," Kishshana says.

Her parents had a vision that she would become a lawyer, get married, and have a family. And that became her vision for herself.

"For much of my early life, I was really trying to just find my way by doing what I thought I was supposed to," she says. She wanted to make her parents proud.

Kishshana earned a bachelor's degree in international relations and a master's in marketing from Bentley University in Massachusetts. She studied and worked abroad. She thought she was heading for a career in a field like international manufacturing or investment banking.

But then there came a point when she realized that she just wasn't prepared to enter the life for which she'd been educating herself. Furthermore, "I didn't really know what I wanted to do."

She knew what other people expected her to do, the things she felt like she *should* do.

"But I don't think I had a good sense of what *I* wanted to do."

That's a feeling many of us encounter in our early twenties. And when Kishshana was in the midst of it, a fundraising job came along.

"I don't think I sought out that role," she says. "I definitely feel like it fell in my lap."

"Cash" was back.

Finding Her Fire

As she started her career in fundraising, Kishshana discovered that the talents that earned her her childhood nickname were still very much present.

"I just love the thrill of the chase—of getting folks who didn't know you to understand something you care about," she says. Fundraising requires getting others to "see themselves in the work you care so deeply about."

She started getting managerial experience early, which taught her "how to really think about what makes people tick, what is it that makes people unique."

It was also educational to work with so many people who were older than she. She learned how to "navigate different generations, working styles, and norms and beliefs and practices" Kishshana says. "It made me a better manager."

Her abilities as a leader opened doors to other roles, and she built an impressive track record of money raised, leaders developed, and lives changed.

Behind those successes, though, there were some painful things to manage.

As she started her career, Kishshana realized the amount of code-switching involved in being a black woman in the workplace. If you're not familiar with that term, it means speaking or presenting yourself one way in your work sphere and another way in your personal sphere. In other words, you don't feel like you can bring your full self to work.

This was a theme that would continue through her subsequent roles.

She remembers how things about her that were considered "fun and interesting and so bright and happy and different" when she interviewed were perceived differently once she'd been around a while. "Oh, cool! You ask a lot of questions!" became "Oh (sigh) you ask A LOT of questions."

"I think that I burnt myself out trying to straddle who I am and how I show up," she says. "I was perfectly coiffed. My diction was tight. I did not hang out with people after work. I really didn't fraternize with folks. I had one life at work, and I had a completely different life at home."

She continues: "I also know now that my co-workers, particularly when I worked in mostly white spaces, didn't really make an effort to include me either. And so it probably was sort of like subconsciously protecting myself but also knowing I have to do the heavy lifting. And I already do a lot of heavy lifting. "

These are issues with which she continues to grapple , even as her path as a #Firestarter veered away from organizational work and into a new phase.

Spreading Her Spark

In 2009, Kishshana decided to build her own movement as a "speaker, educator, trainer, coach, and recovering fundraiser," as she puts it on her website.

Her work is varied. You might find her giving a keynote at an event; leading training sessions for an organization's board, leaders or team members; coaching high performers; helping consultants and business owners rebrand; or guiding organizations through strategic planning or hiring team members.

But she doesn't just spread her know-how through in-person work. She has her own leadership blog (secretlivesofleaders.com) and a wealth of resources (including some freebies) for fellow #Firestarters on her business website. I also recommend that you pick up a copy of her book *Hey, I'm New Here: Advice for Leaders of the New School*, a practical guide for new managers.

Kishshana also understands that #Firestarters need good swag—and as someone with my own online shop, I heartily concur! Kishshana's product brand, The Social Good Life, includes a planner especially for fundraisers as well as *cute* t-shirts and home and office goods to inspire fundraisers and other #Firestarters.

Another project that she's especially excited about is creating Rooted, "an online global community for women of color (WOC) who raise money," she says. "That is work I feel like I was called to do."

She envisions a place where WOC development officials "can come for community; they can come for learning. They can come for a safe space. They can come for mentorship and sponsorship."

Her vision is that Rooted will become 10,000 women strong and that it will transform the missions of the organizations those women serve.

What else does she see in the coming years? Growth for her consulting business and major media coverage. International speaking gigs. Her product line taking on a life of its own. And a thriving future for her daughter, who's in her first year of high school.

"She's my crowning achievement of a human that I have been afforded the gift of guiding her steps until she steps fully into the calling her own life," Kishshana says.

And perhaps that future will include becoming CEO of one of the sub-brands of Kishshana's company someday.

"I think that would be amazing," she says. "It's something she's been thinking a lot about, and so I would be super-excited to support her."

Kishshana's work as a #Firestarter is evolving because *she's* evolving. As a fellow midcareer professional working in social good, I really love Kishshana's insights about how that "movement within" affects the movements we create. For her, that's meant understanding there's a difference between confidence and self-worth.

"I think that many of us, in particular women of color, in particular black women, learned very early on how to have high self-confidence" in terms of the way we look, the way we speak, and the energy we give off, she says.

Those are all things we can practice, she adds. But they're all on the outside. You can be projecting all kinds of confidence to the world, but inside, grading yourself harshly.

"What I had to understand and then decide to do something about was that I had very high self-confidence, and I had very low worth," she says. "And that inner-narrative that I had on loop was so powerful that it was causing me to self-sabotage opportunities because I didn't think I was worthy—even though on the outside I could talk a good game!"

Another big theme for her is pushing herself to her fullest. "I am, by nature, a high achiever," she says. "And so my C is typically many a person's A." But she knows what her own A game really is, and leaning into it is enabling her to do the things—like creating Rooted—that she's truly passionate about.

"I know it is going to change the game in my profession," she says.

"I did not set out to do that. But now that I am doing it, I feel amazing about it."

Ignite Your Own Fire

What can you take away from Kishshana's story to catalyze your own movement?

Start strong

If you're just setting out in your career or in building your movement, understand your value and your strengths—"how those strengths show up for you when you are at your best and how those strengths show up for you when you are protecting yourself."

Find some sponsors

You don't just need mentors, Kishshana stresses. "Getting a sponsor who can really open doors for you *early* is super-important." There are people who have decision-making power because of their titles, and then there are the gatekeepers—the people who can get you access to the decision-makers. "Endear yourself to them in a very authentic way."

Nurture yourself

"Do things that bring you joy, and keep that glimmer of hope in your eye," Kishshana says. "Because that is what you're going to need when things are hard. And every one of us has a season when things are just ridiculously hard."

Get comfortable with speaking up

Know how to name when something is wrong in a way that doesn't put you on the defensive. Kishshana got good at saying things like "I just want to flag that I know that you don't mean (fill in the blank) because you really want the best for me. But I have to tell you what I'm experiencing at this moment is (fill in the blank), and I know you wouldn't do that. Am I right?"

Maximize your giving—or your movement

I asked Kishshana for some tips on how we can all make a bigger difference with the money we give. As I read back over her answers, I realized that her advice on giving also contains a lot of wisdom on creating a successful movement:

- One criterion for choosing where to give is looking for an organization that impacts the community where you live or work, Kishshana says. Similarly, you might not need to look any farther than the people around you to find the inspiration for the movement you are meant to lead.

- Your past experiences, both good and bad, may also shape who you are as a giver or as a #Firestarter. Did a positive experience, like receiving a scholarship, shape who you are? How can you help others share your good fortune? On the other hand, you can also be driven to give or build a movement because you want to spare others a painful experience through which you've gone.

- When you're considering donating to an organization, look at its leadership. Does it reflect the population that the group serves? "That's a really important barometer for me about where I put my money," Kishshana says. And if you're building a movement, remember this as you choose the people who will lead it alongside you.

Amanda Edwards
The Candidate

*"It's not enough for us to talk about problems.
We've got to be a part of the solution."*

A #Firestarter's Beginnings

Over the past few years, Amanda Edwards has worked tirelessly as a city council member to create a brighter, more inclusive future for Houston, a city that the *Los Angeles Times* called "the most diverse place in America."

And, as I write this, she just wrapped-up a campaign seeking to become the Democratic candidate taking on Republican incumbent John Cornyn for his US Senate seat. In a crowded field, Amanda finished in the top five but missed the runoff.

But you're still going to want to keep your eye on Amanda—who has been called a "rising Democratic star" by *The Washington Post.* Amid all the overheated rhetoric that has made so many of us lose faith in the political process, Amanda has the knowledge, the integrity, and the focus to be a powerful agent for change.

Like many of the other women I talked to for this book, Amanda came from a family where service was second nature.

There's always someone who needs help, and there's always a way you *can* help.

"You give back no matter where you are," she says. She believes in pushing yourself to be the best person you can be and, in the process, helping your community be at its best.

It was a crisis within her family that showed Amanda the real stakes of politics.

When she was ten, her father was diagnosed with cancer. As a tween and a teen, she learned some hard truths about our country's health-care system that many of us don't have to consider until adulthood.

"I began to ask him lots of questions about health care and things like that," she says. "And I just thought it was incredibly crazy."

Because he had insurance coverage, her father had access to treatments that gave him several more years with his family after his diagnosis. He passed away when Amanda was seventeen. She thinks a lot about the life lessons he was able to share with her in those years—and how she might have missed them if he had lacked health coverage.

"That was my first introduction to the real purpose behind policy," she says. "This is real-life stuff. It isn't just a political game."

Here's something else that touched my heart about Amanda's teen years: Even amid her father's illness, her family encouraged her to be bold in going after her dreams.

At her Houston high school, "it was not expected of us necessarily to go to the Ivy League, to go very far away for school." But Amanda had other ideas and aimed high as she applied to colleges.

"I remember having a conversation with my dad," she says. "And I said 'Well, can I go?… If I get into all of these schools, is that something I can do? Would you be okay with that?'"

"But there were no limits placed on me by my parents," she continues. They told her, "Just go as high as you can go. Go for it, and we'll support you."

She knows what a big deal that was.

"It never occurred to me that I shouldn't be pursuing anything I wanted to pursue," she says.

And what she pursued was impressive: Amanda earned a political science degree from the prestigious Emory University in Atlanta where she also served as undergraduate student body president. She later received her JD degree from Harvard Law School.

As she worked on her education, Amanda was also gaining experiences that would lay the foundation for her future career. While at Emory, she worked in community development corporations and in the Georgia State Legislature. She learned the importance of creating buy-in and of being flexible enough to change her approach. At one time, she even blogged for Elizabeth Warren!

"It's so important that you understand how to work with communities properly," she says. "There's a difference between imposing on a community and being invited in and working alongside."

Another pivotal experience for Amanda was relocating to New Orleans in the aftermath of Hurricane Katrina. "I felt compelled to move there," she says.

She worked as a clerk for a federal judge, and she founded a program called Project NOW: The New Orleans Writing Project.

"I got an opportunity to really make a difference in the lives of young people by teaching them how to use writing as a tool of empowerment after the storm," she says. "It was such a rewarding experience to be able to contribute in a meaningful way."

While Amanda had already accomplished so much by this point, there was so much more ahead for her.

Finding Her Fire

After her time in New Orleans, Amanda returned home to Houston to practice law. In 2015, she decided to seek a seat on Houston's city council.

"I ran because it was time for me not to be a spectator," she says. "It's not enough for us to talk about problems. We've got to be a part of the solution."

Amanda was elected to the council and served a constituency of 2.3 million people. Her work centered on building a bright future for Houston, and people were noticing. It was often said that Amanda would one day serve as Houston mayor. She was passionate about issues like promoting innovation and improving transportation.

"I've really focused on being a forward-thinking leader," she says. As a leader, it's easy to get consumed by the crises in front of you and not be able to focus on your longer-term vision. "You've got to do the immediate things that have to get done and that you have to respond to, but you've also got to keep yourself focused on how to make the community better and have the opportunities that will make this community continue to thrive and push even further."

Her early experiences in community development were valuable as she worked to make sure that all of Houston's communities are a part of the city's progress and that Houston preserves what makes it unique even as it changes.

"We've got a lot of people who live in areas that have been under-resourced," she says. "So how do we responsibly re-infuse investment opportunities in those communities without displacing residents?"

During Amanda's term, Houston experienced one of the most devastating events in its history: Hurricane Harvey in 2017.

"We're not out of the woods yet with recovery at all," she says. "I want to see us do a much more resident-centric recovery process."

Spreading Her Spark

In 2019, Amanda decided to extend her future-forward vision beyond Houston. She announced her run for US Senate on July 18 of that year. Health-care access, the topic that first sparked her interest in politics, was one of the key issues in her campaign. At the time of our interview, Amanda's mother faced the same battle her husband did years ago: a cancer diagnosis. With her family's story as inspiration, Amanda is also convinced that the political process can serve Americans a whole lot better than it does now.

"It's important that we restore our government back to the people," she says. "We've got to have deliverables that transform people's lives."

She realizes that a lot of people feel disconnected from political discourse and that they don't believe their voices matter. We're more used to seeing political sniping on Twitter than we are used to seeing government improving our lives, Amanda says.

"I think it's very dangerous for our nation to have politics get to this level," she says. Something has to change.

"You can't be about the rhetoric," she says. "We have to be about more than that, which is producing results for people. I think that is going to be imperative in this particular election cycle."

From her council work, she's seen that a lot of getting results comes down to just being open and present. In other words, you shouldn't only see or hear from your elected officials at election time.

"I consider my relationship with my residents to be a partnership," she says. "You're telling me what you need, and I'm sharing with you what you need to know. Those two things have to happen in order for civic engagement to be in the right balance."

Ignite Your Own Fire

What can you take away from Amanda's story to catalyze your own movement?

The big question

Thinking about following Amanda's lead and running for office? There's one important thing to ask yourself first before you decide to enter politics: Is this about you or about what you can do for others? (If you're reading this book, I'm confident about what your answer is going to be.) If you're in it just for yourself, politics isn't for you, Amanda says.

The OTHER big question

Now that you're sure that you're running for office to serve others, think about whether you've got what it takes to really make a difference for them. Being an effective elected official requires more than just having a lot of opinions, Amanda says. And it even takes more than having a heart to serve. You also need the skills and the know-how to make the changes you want to see happen. That means you might need to get some training or experiences in different areas before you seek office so that you accomplish everything you want to do.

Get ready for scrutiny

As you prepare to seek office, there's one more important thing to do, Amanda says. Get your personal house in order. After you become a candidate, others are going to be scrutinizing you, so it's a whole lot easier to scrutinize yourself first. That doesn't mean you should strive for perfection, but it does mean that you want to live with purpose, transparency, and consistency. You know the saying, "Walk the walk."

You don't need permission

But what if you're already good to go on all of this? You know what you want to accomplish by running, you have the expertise to do it, *and* you're prepared on a personal level? "Then go for it," Amanda says. "And don't wait for anybody to ask."

Don't limit your dreams

Whether you aspire to run for office or not, Amanda wants to give you the same kind of encouragement her parents gave her. "Don't tell yourself 'no,'" she says. "You let other people do that for you. When they do, and it will happen, then learn your lessons from that."

"You won't blow up; you won't die if you're rejected," she continues. "So don't be fearful of rejection in pursuit of your goals. And don't limit your goals. You're only going to go as far as your imagination will let you."

Amanda is proof that it takes faith and fortitude to accomplish your wildest dreams. That's always been one of the reasons I've admired Amanda as an elected official and female leader, but, most importantly, as a human.

9

Ashley Cheng
The Founder

"I realized I could and should be doing a lot more."

A #Firestarter's Beginnings

Today, Ashley Cheng works for political change as co-founder of the Rouser communications firm and co-host of *The Rabble* podcast. She can trace her interest in politics to her college days at Boston University. But the path from her college activism to her current career wasn't a direct one.

Back in college, Ashley worked passionately on John Kerry's 2004 presidential campaign and volunteered at the Democratic National Convention in Boston. She was all in.

And then her candidate lost to George W. Bush.

"I was just so devastated and taken back," she says. "I was just so young. It was my first time ever voting in a presiden-tial election, and then to have it not go my way. I guess I just gave up right then, really."

In her disappointment, Ashley decided to refocus on her career. (Writing about this part of Ashley's story feels like déjà vu for me. Ashley's journey is so similar to my own: I worked on a US Senate campaign that lost and then pivoted to my current career as a lob-byist.) After majoring in communications at Boston University, Ashley worked in agencies and later as a freelance communications strategist and consultant. She built expertise in areas like event marketing, media strategy, and influencer campaigns. Ashley pursued other passions as well. She became a certified yoga instructor and co-founded Austin School of Yoga. And she launched an ice cream shop, SPUN, with her sister.

Through the years, she still paid attention to the news and voted in major elections, and she gave back to the community as vice president and communications chair of Slow Food Austin (an organization that works to reconnect people with origins of the foods they eat), a role she still holds. But political activism wasn't the big part of her life that it had been in college.

That brings us up to 2016 and another presidential election that left Ashley disappointed and reeling when it was all over. She was haunted by guilt that she hadn't stayed active in politics after college.

"I had had this spark in me to want to get more involved at some point," she says. "And I gave up so easily."

She was also struck by the fact that although she had grown up in Texas, she knew very little about local and state government.

"I had a moment when I realized I could and should be doing a lot more," she says.

Finding Her Fire

Doing more and learning more became Ashley's new mission.

"I spent all of my spare time showing up to events and asking people questions about how things worked and how to get involved," she says.

As Ashley started attending more and more events that aligned with her political beliefs, she kept running into Becky Bullard, another marketing and communications pro. As the two became friends, they mused about how great it would be if they could spend all of their time on the activism they were so passionate about—if it could somehow become their job.

Ashley and Becky decided to host a fundraiser for Kim Olson, who was running for Texas agriculture commissioner.

"We had a blast," Ashley says. And Olson was thrilled with their work.

"She turned to us and was like, 'We need more women like you doing the work,'" Ashley says.

She and Becky took Olson's words at that moment to heart. All of their "What if this were our job?" talks began to seem a lot more real.

Olson's encouragement helped spur Ashley, Becky, and Kristen Gunn, their third business partner, to launch Rouser. Olson became their first client.

So what does it look like when your "what if…"becomes a reality?

Through Rouser, Ashley, Becky, and Kristen use their well-honed communications skills to bring more people into a political process that can feel intimidating and that can shut people out. They provide, as Ashley describes it, "straightforward messaging to normal people like us."

Like Rouser, *The Rabble* podcast came into existence because Ashley, Becky, and Kristen identified a need and saw that they could fill it.

"It was difficult for us to find a media source, specifically about Texas politics, that felt like it was speaking to us as women and as newbies to political activism," Ashley says.

They wanted to not just find out what's going on in politics but also get ideas for how they could take action while inspiring others to act as well. After all, as Ashley points out, it's disheartening to find out about a problem or an issue and then have to take the time to research the best ways to help.

They kept telling others about their idea for the podcast and encouraging them to start it, but they couldn't find anyone else willing to take the idea and run with it.

"So we finally decided 'I guess we just do this ourselves,'" Ashley says.

The trio divides their time between creating content for the podcast and working on branding and messaging with clients like Olson, who became a candidate for Congress from Texas House District 24. At the time we spoke, Rouser's other recent projects included getting the word out about the 2020 Census to ensure that communities of color are counted accurately and working on a fundraiser with Blue Action Democrats.

"We get to support a lot of the work we believe in Texas," she says.

The women of Rouser had also just emceed a Superlocal event for Supermajority, an organization bringing women together to build economic and political power. Ashley was awed and grateful that only a few months after starting their podcast, they were sharing the stage with the founders of Superlocal: Alicia Garza of Black Lives Matter; Ai-Jen Poo of the National Domestic Workers Alliance; and Cecile Richards, former Planned Parenthood president. And after attending so many events that had galvanized her own activism, it also meant a lot to Ashley to have her chance to inspire and inform others.

Spreading Her Spark

All of Ashley's work with Rouser and *The Rabble* advances the same underlying mission. She and her partners want to "mobilize people in Texas and get them educated about the issues and what's happening right now but also get them really confident about how their own voice has value and how their own unique lived experience is so essential to the wider story of Texas."

As this happens, Ashley hopes to see a more diverse group of people running for office in Texas so that the state's leadership more accurately reflects its population. She hopes that the work of Rouser and *The Rabble* helps build the "bench strength" of future leaders in Texas.

"They know that they have a voice in it and that their voice matters," Ashley says. "The system wasn't built for us, but we can be rebuilt by all of us."

Ignite Your Own Fire

What can you take away from Ashley's story to catalyze your own movement?

So let us ask you something...

Have you considered seeking a political office but feel hesitant? You're not alone, Ashley says. Typically, it takes getting asked to run for office seven times for a woman to enter a race. If you're reading this, Ashley says, she's asking you to run. So that's one request. I'm going to join her, so now you've been asked twice. And, hey, why wait around for those other five requests? You've got things to accomplish!

Get out there

If you aren't sure if you want to get into politics but you know you still want to work for change, a great first step is to just start going to events that interest you and asking questions. This is exactly what helped lead Ashley to her current career with Rouser and *The Rabble*. Feel a little hesitant about asking those questions? Ashley can identify.

"I've always been so timid," she says. "Growing up, I was never the first person to raise my hand."

So what helped her overcome her self-consciousness?

"I realized how meaningful these connections were that I could make when I'm willing to speak out," she says.

Remember, if you're thinking something, someone else is too.

When you find the courage to say it, you're empowering her to speak her mind as well.

And if that's not enough, you should know that just being in the audience works too. Those who are speaking, running for office or starting a rally need people to get out there and show up.

Share your story

It doesn't just take courage to speak up and show up at events, though. Sometimes talking about politics or hot-button issues with the people close to us can require even more bravery.

If you're not sure how to connect with others over the issues you care about, sharing a personal story is one of the most powerful ways to communicate.

"It's hard to argue with someone's lived experience," Ashley says. "If we can get ourselves to the place where we stop dehumanizing one another, I think that's the only we can really have these conversations and not just end up shouting."

At the same time, listen respectfully when others share their experiences. You don't have to agree with them, but thank them for telling their stories.

Don't worry about sounding 'smart'

One of the first things you'll notice about Rouser and *The Rabble* is that Ashley and her co-founders speak to their audience in relatable, everyday language. There's not a political buzzword visible to the eye or one that the ear will hear.

"If you're starting out in this work and trying to build these movements, there is constantly that annoying gnat of imposter syndrome buzzing at your side," she says. "And that's what fuels us to use jargon and [to] try to sound quote-unquote smarter. But at the end of the day, no one wants to be spoken to like that. It's about finding your own voice and using it…. It's going to resonate so much better with other people. We all just want to be spoken to as humans."

Anger + joy = awesome activism

As you start figuring out how you want to make a difference, Ashley has a formula that can help: Use what brings you the most joy to take on what angers you the most.

Take Ashley's business partner, Kristen. She loves creating art, and she's enraged by family separations at the Texas-Mexico border, so she used her artistic talents to create murals around Austin to raise awareness of the border crisis.

Do more than nothing

Need an even simpler formula? Ashley gets where you're coming from, and so do I. All of us go through times when all the problems in the world feel overwhelming and your own capacity feels small. When you aren't sure how you could possibly make a difference or where to even start, let this be your mantra: Do more than nothing. (Ashley credits *The Rabble* guest Stephanie Chiarello, for this wisdom.)

Fire up another woman

Here's one more super-easy thing you can do. One of the pivotal moments in the story of Rouser and *The Rabble* was when Kim Olson told the team how much she believed in them and how needed were their efforts. Think about the other women in your world. Who makes you think "Now *she* could change the world"? Tell her—be part of her story! You could be just the spark she needs to become a #Firestarter in her own right.

Karen Hansen
The Survivor

"I show them that they don't have to be a victim."

A #Firestarter's Beginnings

Like many of the other women in this book, Karen Hansen became the #Firestarter she is today in part because of the influence of her early experiences. In Karen's case, however, those experiences are painful to recall.

"I kind of was always like a black sheep of my family," she says of growing up in the small town of Leesburg, Florida. "So I always felt like I couldn't relate to anyone within my family."

Karen felt like she had been misplaced. "As a child, I was consistently told I was a 'challenge' and that I would never amount to anything," she says.

Even her physical environment felt wrong. This future interior designer was raised in cluttered, chaotic spaces but always craved cleanliness and organization.

But the most devastating part of Karen's early years was that she was a victim of childhood sexual assault.

"You don't know that that's not normal" as a child, she says. "But you feel like something's wrong." And she didn't know whom she could tell because the very people hurting her were the ones who were supposed to protect her.

While Karen says her childhood led to her becoming the resilient woman she is today, she also feels that it made her more vulnerable as a young adult. When she was studying interior design at Florida State University, Karen was the victim of date rape and became pregnant.

Even as she became a young mother and carried a traumatic secret with her, Karen completed her education and launched her career as a designer. After moving to Boca Raton, Florida, she got to know another young woman who would change the course of her life: Laura Rachlin.

If ever two people were fated to meet, Karen and Laura were. Laura was another small-town Florida girl who had studied interior design at FSU, though she and Karen did not know each other during college. They didn't meet until both had moved to Boca Raton, but when they did—during an industry event—they hit it off fast. Eventually, the two became colleagues, and they then went out on their own to start a commercial interior design business, In.design, together. The timing was challenging. The two young moms had to hold that fledgling business together in the aftermath of the September 11, 2001 attacks when the nation was reeling both psychologically and economically.

As they grew their firm together, Karen and Laura also discovered that they had more in common than their love of the same profession. Like Karen, Laura was carrying the trauma of being date-raped when she was at FSU. And the two women would have to weather more painful times together. Laura's former husband, the father of her three children, was abusive. Soon after their divorce in 2013, he took his own life. Karen experienced domestic violence in her own marriage, and her then-husband sexually abused her daughter.

That's *a lot*—enough to break anyone's spirit—but they were determined that their past experiences would not dictate the rest of their lives. Karen and Laura were resolved to rise above—for their kids, for their business, and for themselves. They are the perfect examples of fuel for #Firestarters.

Finding Her Fire

After all they had been through, it's only natural that Karen and Laura found themselves in a reflective mood a few years ago.

They thought about all of the trauma they had survived, but they also thought about their blessings, like their thriving business and the great people that surrounded them.

"Why is it that all of these bad things have happened, and why have all these good things happened?" Karen remembers wondering. And what were they supposed to do with it all?

Karen and Laura figured they had two choices. They could simply revel in their own success, or they could turn both the bad things and the good things that had happened to them into a movement about empowerment and being a survivor. They could be a voice for those who had not found theirs yet.

And they had a unique way to do this. In addition to their interior design firm, Karen and Laura were also pursuing a new passion: launching their own handbag line, Wren & Roch (inspired by their names).

They decided to contribute a portion of all sales to organizations that help victims of sexual assault. And the Wren & Roch website isn't just a place to shop for beautiful accessories; it also educates visitors on sexual assault and domestic violence and the resources available to help them if they're being victimized.

Karen and Laura created the Wren & Roch Foundation to help spread their message of abuse awareness and prevention. They've spoken to countless people, from the White House to the United Nations and all kinds of events in between. As they began to share their stories, both women and men began to tell them their own stories of sexual assault—stories that were unspeakably horrible.

"I'm a very sensitive person," Karen says. "Even though in my daily life, everyone thinks that I'm very strong, but I really tend to take on others' pain."

To process everything that she was hearing, Karen went to therapy. She realized that it's not possible for her to heal someone from a long-carried trauma in just a passing conversation, but she also realized what she *can* do—and it's a lot. She encourages the people who share their stories with her to seek therapy themselves and to work through their pain by journaling.

"I show them what a survivor can look like," she says. "I show them that they don't have to be a victim and that that might be where they *were*, but they don't have to do that forever." She wants the people she meets to know that they can thrive and excel, just as she and Laura have.

Karen also shares statistics so that other survivors of sexual assault know that they're not alone.

"I let them know that I'm sorry that that happened to them and that it's not their fault," she says. That's important because many victims blame themselves.

The tagline of their brand is "carry your courage," and that's exactly what Karen and Laura help their fellow survivors do. In doing so, they also *stop* carrying around any guilt and shame.

Spreading Her Spark

Karen continues the hard work of being a #Firestarter because we still have a long way to go in preventing sexual assault and in being more compassionate toward its survivors.

"I think the first thing is just being able to talk about it," she says. By telling her story, she empowers others to tell theirs. All keeping silent does is "encourage more of that behavior because the victim is the one walking around filled with shame, not the predator."

She also wants Wren & Roch's movement to help *finally* put a stop to victim-blaming. Even today, far too many people look first for something that the victim was "doing wrong" that "caused" the sexual assault to happen.

"I don't care if you're drunk, walking down the street naked, you don't deserve for that to happen to you, and no one should touch you no matter what," she says.

To sustain their movement, Karen and Laura are working on growing their company and creating new products. They also want to explore what else they can do with their foundation.

As Karen and Laura look toward what's next for their business and their movement, their partnership is still going strong. Twenty-year business partnerships are rare enough on their own, but Karen and Laura are also still best friends. They make every decision together, and they even share an office. When one is having a bad day, the other carries her. "We rely on each other a lot," Karen says. And they're a legacy they're proud of through both their design work and their advocacy.

"I have made it my personal goal to know that the day I die it will have mattered that I was on this Earth and that I contributed to it in a meaningful, positive way," Karen says.

Ignite Your Own Fire

What can you take away from Karen's story to catalyze your own movement?

Ignore the naysayers

Karen has achieved everything that she has after being told as a kid that she would never amount to anything. "Don't let anyone tell you what you can't do," she says. "The only thing standing between you and your dreams is you." Believe in your gifts, talents and your ability to change your life—and the world.

Dare to share your dream

You don't have to do everything on your own, #Firestarter. "Don't be afraid to ask for help," Karen says. "What you'll find is a lot of people who will actually take action and try to help you achieve those dreams. If you keep them to yourself, how is anyone ever going to know that they could help you?"

Lift up other women

We can all support each other, Karen says. "We are so much stronger together, and there's just no point in being catty."

Take self-care seriously

You're a #Firestarter, not a martyr. The point isn't to give so much that you deplete yourself. The reason that Karen can keep on being there for the people who want to share their stories with her is that she replenishes herself through therapy. What do you need on a personal level to make your movement sustainable?

Transform your pain

Karen is a reminder of how we can find the seeds of a movement in even our greatest traumas. Like her, you may want to try having a "What I am supposed to do with this?" conversation with a trusted friend or even with yourself.

Tishaura Jones
The Elected

"We're playing the long game here. How many lives can we change over the long term?"

A #Firestarter's Beginnings

Politics is in the blood of Tishaura Jones, St. Louis city treasurer. Her father served as comptroller for St. Louis, but that doesn't mean she grew up aspiring to hold office—or believing that if she did that everything would be handed to her.

"I never really thought that I would get into politics. You never want to do what your parents do," she says with a laugh.

So, instead, Tishaura got a bachelor's degree in finance from Hampton University in Virginia and a master's in health administration from Saint Louis University. As she was building a career outside of politics, though, crises in her family would set the stage for her own eventual move into public service.

Her father was sentenced to eight months in prison for tax evasion. For most children, having your father away would be traumatic enough, but the universe would add to Tishaura's plate. "And then shortly after he returned from prison, my mother became gravely ill and subsequently passed away," Tishaura says.

As an only child, Tishaura was taking care of her mother and managing her father's affairs while he was imprisoned. "Bills piled up, and I had to file bankruptcy," she says.

With everything that was going on in her life, Tishaura didn't go looking for opportunities in politics. Instead, the opportunity came to find her. A committeeperson spot became open for the city's 8th Ward, and she was asked to fill the volunteer role.

"And it was that appointment that sort of awakened some latent DNA in my genetic makeup," she says. "I started meeting a whole host of people and seeing how politics changes lives if done the right way."

Tishaura was going from "Politics? No way!" to "I could really see myself doing this." And she began to think she might enjoy it while changing the lives of people she saw as neighbors or as friends.

Finding Her Fire

She continued in the committeeperson role for six years and then ran for the Missouri House of Representatives. "I won my first time out of the box, and I've been in politics ever since," she says.

As a legislator, she was passionate about health care and health policy. As the single mother of a young child, she also worked to create positive change in education and economic development.

Because her party was in the minority in the House, Tishaura knew she had to build strong relationships to make things happen. She even broke from her fellow Democratic Party lawmakers some-times, such as when she sponsored a bill letting charter schools expand statewide while increasing their accountability. "I'm an advo-cate for good education no matter where children get it from," she says. It was decisions such as this one to step up as a leader that got Tishaura noticed by many.

It was in the legislature, Tishaura was elected assistant minority floor leader—the first woman and the first African American to hold this position in Missouri.

She didn't know when she took on this role that she was making history. Finding out about the milestone she had achieved was pretty cool. But, at the same time, she took the responsibility very seriously. "I knew I would be in rooms and at tables that a lot of people wouldn't necessarily be at," she says. "I chose to exert my voice and use my voice to help my people and to advocate and campaign for things that matter."

One moment she remembers is joining the minority leader to speak with the governor about an abortion bill she opposed. "I don't know if what I said led him to veto it or some other things, but shortly thereafter, he did veto the bill," she says.

After serving in the State House, Tishaura was elected St. Louis city treasurer in 2012. Her work in this role is a powerful reminder of just how much local politics affects our lives—and of what one determined #Firestarter can accomplish as a local leader.

As treasurer, Tishaura is the city's chief investment and cash management officer as well as its parking supervisor. Remembering what it was like to rebuild her credit and her life after her family's crises, she's now dedicated to helping others take control of their own finances. To do that, Tishaura started the Office of Financial Empowerment.

"We provide free financial coaching and counseling to anybody who walks in, and they don't have to be a city resident," she says. Participants learn about a variety of topics such as how to repair their credit or have their federal student loans forgiven.

One of the most exciting programs is College Kids, which sets up a savings account with $50 for every kindergartner in St. Louis public schools. "That program is four years old and we have over 13,500 children saving for college as a result of starting this program," she says.

Besides adding to their accounts themselves, families can also grow their balances over time through attendance incentives, matched savings, and parents' participation in financial education courses.

Every little bit helps. Even having less than $500 saved dramatically increases a child's chances of enrolling in and graduating from college someday. And then there's something you can't put a dollar value on: Just knowing that city leaders care about their future gives kids hope and encouragement, Tishaura says.

"We're playing the long game here," she says. "How many lives can we change over the long term?"

The money for College Kids comes from donations and from residual parking revenue. "I'm always reminding people when they get a parking ticket, 'You know you're helping kids, right?'" she says with a laugh.

Seeing the impact of her work—like when children and parents thank her for the savings accounts—keeps Tishaura going through the challenging times that are inevitably part of being a #Firestarter. For example, not everyone is happy with her office's handling of residual parking funds, and when I talked with Tishaura last summer, this was actually the subject of a lawsuit before the Missouri Supreme Court.

Another one of her biggest challenges was when she decided to run for St. Louis mayor in 2017 and lost the Democratic primary by fewer than one-thousand votes. It was a bruising election. "All of my dirty laundry was aired by the local press, and none of the dirty laundry of any of the other candidates was," she told the podcast *The 23%: Conversations With Women in Government* in 2018. "So I felt this was a concerted effort to, dare I say, keep a black woman down."

Her letter about the *St. Louis Post-Dispatch's* coverage of her campaign went viral after it was published in the *St. Louis American*, the city's African American newspaper.

In the aftermath of the election, Tishaura even considered leaving St. Louis, but she didn't want to let her team down, and she wanted to keep growing programs like College Kids.

Spreading Her Spark

There's so much Tishaura still wants to accomplish for St. Louis.

She envisions expanding her education programs to guarantee either two or four years of college or community college for all graduates of the city's public high schools. She also wants to ensure that all new high school graduates receive a copy of their credit report as well as information on the importance of protecting their credit scores.

Another possibility for her future is running for mayor again. "I see the potential that St. Louis has if we are just smart about the decisions we make with our public dollars: Finding the root cause of the crime instead of just throwing more cops in the mix, putting the right mix of public safety there with social workers, and other mental health and substance abuse professionals."

She also points to the need for investment in "neighborhoods that have seen no investment in decades" and for closing the racial wealth divide by creating more opportunities for homeownership among low-income people and people of color.

St. Louis is at a crossroads right now, and Tishaura wants to "be there and watch it turn the corner and return to a place that people want to move to."

Ignite Your Own Fire

What can you take away from Tishaura's story to catalyze your own movement?

Help is out there

If you are thinking about getting into politics, you don't have to figure everything out on your own. "There are several great programs and organizations out there that will help give you the information you need to make that leap," she says. One is VoteRunLead

(voterunlead.org), which trains women to run for office and win. Tishaura is one of the organization's certified trainers. She's also a fan of Higher Heights (higherheightsforamerica.org), which builds the pipeline of black women leaders.

Get a mentor

Like so many other women in this book, Tishaura affirms that #Firestarters need mentors—and not just at the beginning of their careers. She deeply values the people in her life today who can answer her questions and who can give it to her straight.

Take time to recharge

When you're dedicated to your movement, it's easy to neglect caring for yourself. That's just not sustainable, though. Tishaura didn't take a vacation during her first two years as city treasurer. But now she's much more vigilant about protecting time for herself and time spent with her son.

It's okay to cry

"There were times early in my career where I would cry over the slightest thing, especially in the legislature," Tishaura says. These days, she takes things less personally. "But I would also say don't become so hard that you think crying is a weakness," she says. "Allow yourself the space and opportunity to have feelings about the things you are passionate about and the things you are working toward."

If you read my blog, you know that I didn't learn to express emotions until later in life. It was actually after my father died when I really opened myself in this manner. I call it "The Movement Within." #Firestarters, if we aren't healthy, whole, and authentic inside, any movement we try to build will fall flat. The movement inside of each of us fuels us, so it's important to bring it to our work.

'Winning isn't everything'

All #Firestarters run into defeat sometimes, but that doesn't have to derail your movement. "There is life after a loss," Tishaura says. I must say that this is music to my ears. So many times as women we are taught that we must be successful. It's important to realize that there will be wins and losses. The roller coaster of life is clear from Tishaura's story, but the silver lining of her defeat in the mayoral election was that she could devote more time to her young son. She also realized that she still had influence to exert in city government. "Even though I lost, I still feel like I have a voice and that voice matters," she says. "Winning isn't everything."

'Be your authentic self'

One of Tishaura's greatest insights for rising #Firestarters comes from one of the hardest times in her life: the 2017 mayoral race. Typically, local candidates do an interview with the *Post-Dispatch* editorial board, but based on their coverage of her, Tishaura didn't see the value in sitting down with the newspaper. Right up until the morning the interview was scheduled, she went back and forth with her team over whether it should happen. She felt pushed to the brink.

"I don't know if this will classify as a nervous breakdown, but it was pretty darn close," she says.

After talking to her father, she decided that she just could not subject herself to the interview. Instead, she wrote the viral letter that appeared in the *St. Louis American*.

"I want other women of color to see from my example that it is okay to be your authentic self," Tishaura says. "It's okay to say 'no' to things you don't want to do and that don't sit right with your spirit." You are the only person who can tell your story from a place of authenticity, experience, and loyalty.

#Firestarters, I personally feel that many times we get on a hamster wheel and chase the carrot that others hold in front of us. We grow numb to knowing if it is what we really want or what will make us happy. Instead, take a moment to think if it is the very thing that will allow you to speak your truth. Tishaura did that, and it paid off, and I have a feeling it will continue to in her bright future.

Tatiana Torres
The Amplifier

"I turned that sadness into zeal and passion."

A #Firestarter's Beginnings

Today Tatiana Torres passionately stands up for the underserved and the underheard. This sense of mission has its roots in her early childhood.

Tatiana was born in Colombia. Her mother worked in the department of education, and her father was an air force pilot with an interest in politics, public service, and social justice. He was even studying for a second degree in journalism.

This was during the '80s, the era of drug lord Pablo Escobar and the Medellin Cartel. Her father was threatened because he would not join the drug trade.

"He would have died," Tatiana says. "And he wanted to see his kids grow up with a father since he had not been raised with one."

So her family decided to seek asylum in the US. Tatiana was four, and her life became very different, very quickly. They went from a beautiful home in Colombia to a tiny apartment in a small

New Jersey town about fifteen minutes from New York City. At the time, they were the only Latino family there.

In Colombia, it was affordable to hire household helpers. When they got to New Jersey, Tatiana remembers asking where her nanny was. Before they had to flee Colombia, her parents had professional careers. In the US, "I've seen them scrub floors and clean toilets for my entire upbringing," she says.

With her parents working so hard, Tatiana and her siblings didn't get to have family dinners with them, but her parents did make sure they had time together on the weekends. And the family spent that time being #Firestarters. They would head for a wholesale club, buy food, and then drive to the inner-city to give those groceries away to people in need. She also remembers hosting missionaries at their house.

Because of her family's influence, Tatiana always had a strong social consciousness, and her political awareness only expanded as a broadcast journalism major at Montclair State University in New Jersey. This happened through both her studies and her activism.

"I began to see the issues that my parents might have not talked about so bluntly in college and see other Latinos that had struggled worse than I had," she says.

While in college, Tatiana was mentored by Nilda Pimentel, who ran Latino and faith-based outreach for New Jersey governors Jon Corzine and Jim McGreevey. Since Tatiana was still undocumented, she couldn't work on a campaign, but Pimentel "took me under her arm and told me everything that I know" about politics and its intersection with faith and media.

After Tatiana was allowed to start working, her first job in politics was serving as special assistant to Washington, DC Council Chairman Kwame Brown. She moved on to a couple of other jobs in Washington before an offer came along that would change her life.

Finding Her Fire

Through a mutual friend, Tatiana became connected with Cheryl Mills, who served as deputy White House counsel for President Bill Clinton and counselor and chief of staff for Hillary Clinton when she was secretary of state. Through Mills, Tatiana learned that Hillary Clinton's 2016 presidential campaign needed a regional director in South Florida. She applied for the job and was selected.

For Tatiana, the new role felt like coming full circle. When her father was a pilot in Colombia, he had traveled with the president of that country. And now she was convinced that she was working for the future President of the United States.

She loved working on the campaign—which made Clinton's loss to Donald Trump in the election all the more painful. She vividly recalls the campaign "boiler room" growing quiet as results from different states came in.

"I left crying," she says. And she wasn't the only one. The next morning, she thought she had dreamt it all, but then reality sank in.

"It was as if someone had died," Tatiana says. She had to work on closing down the campaign office while processing her own grief—and seeing the fear that immigrant families like hers had of the incoming administration. She recalls sitting on the beach in Miami with her fellow campaign staffers, taking solace in the ocean they had never had time to enjoy before because they were working so hard.

Since then, there's been plenty to keep her pain fresh.

"This president does something every day that irks me," Tatiana says. "It reminds me every day why I stay angry."

Spreading Her Spark

You had better believe, though, that Tatiana is going to channel that anger.

"I stay angry because it fuels the passion within me," she says. "There are people that are being treated unjustly. People of color are being suppressed yet again."

She remains fiercely committed to helping the underserved and the vulnerable.

"I turned that sadness into zeal and passion," Tatiana says. "And not just now while he's president. It has to continue—because this will happen again if it doesn't."

She lived out that passion as director of community affairs and social impact—National Capital Area for CareFirst BlueCross BlueShield. Her responsibilities included managing a sponsorship budget of $38 million with her team that supports over two hundred organizations in the Washington, DC area.

"I wanted to go away from politics for a while but wanted to do something that could help people that were going to be impacted by his presidency," she says. The job held extra meaning for her because she remembers her parents having to use payment plans for the family's medical care because they lacked insurance.

And I fully expect her to make a huge impact in her latest role. As director of external engagement—Economic Recovery Unit, DMPED-District of Columbia, she will help DC recover from the coronavirus crisis.

She also continues to be an activist on other fronts. When we talked in late summer 2019, the border crisis was very much on her mind as it loomed large in the national conversation. In December 2018, Tatiana visited a detention camp for women and children in Dilley, Texas.

What does she want others to understand about asylum seekers? "Most of the people that are coming now are women and children," she says. They're fleeing domestic violence in fear for their lives.

History will remember how the US responds to the border crisis and how it treats undocumented immigrants, Tatiana says.

"Why are we not, as the US, paying attention to this cry for help?" she says. That's not synonymous with opening the borders, she says. She believes the first priority should be securing the fate of Deferred Action for Childhood Arrivals (DACA) immigrants.

"These are people that are Americans, like me," she says. "I think that we have to talk about the generation that's being wiped out intentionally—that are Americans, that if they were going to go back to their countries, they wouldn't even know the language."

She stresses something that gets forgotten all too often: This should be a bipartisan issue.

"I think we have to tone down the yelling and do more action and do more talking," Tatiana says. "Stop talking in circles and talk more directly to one another."

Inclusivity also must be a theme for the eventual Democratic presidential nominee, Tatiana told me. (She worked briefly with the Michael Bloomberg presidential nomination campaign before he left the race.)

As a lifelong evangelical Christian, she says Democrats could do better in reaching out to this community.

"You can never forget that there's a new generation of evangelicals that are not here to judge homosexuality and are not here to judge abortion—to be those two-issue voters," she says. "We're very different. Social justice is a big thing for us. I would tell the nominee to engage the evangelical community in a way that they never have before. There are a lot of votes that are being lost."

The candidate must also "engage communities of color right away," Tatiana says. "I would talk about the issues that are suffocating communities of color." No matter the race of the eventual nominee, they need to lead a national conversation about racial equity.

Finally, "I would say make sure that you actually give a damn about the people that you want to represent and make sure that you show it," she says. "It's about actually understanding the needs that there are in many different communities across the country."

So would Tatiana ever consider running for office herself? It's something she can definitely imagine doing. Before she does, though, she'd like to be married and perhaps have a child.

"I know what the political sphere is like, and I know how difficult it is," she says. "And if you don't have someone that you can come home to and ground you, you could lose your mind, and you can lose your compass."

Whether or not she holds elected office, she has a clear vision of the kind of world she wants to work for. In her vision, more women and people of color are represented in boardrooms. More people are empowered to speak and are involved in making the decisions that affect all of our lives.

"I also would like my legacy to be one of a woman of faith that is not judgmental," Tatiana says. "A woman that reached out to all people, that was the embodiment of social justice and the embodiment of understanding racial equity, and giving a voice to the voiceless."

Ignite Your Own Fire

What can you take away from Tatiana's story to catalyze your own movement?

'Know who you are first'

Tatiana has some real talk for you, young #Firestarters. "It's okay to fall in love and do all that, but you need to know who you are first and what you want as a young lady," she says. Remember also that you have so much value to offer beyond your appearance. Tatiana *isn't* saying never go shopping or get your nails done. She just wants you to prioritize who you are mentally and spiritually.

"Your beauty does have to come from inside, and you have to believe in yourself."

Listen, learn, and have a thick skin

Real talk, part two: It's time to build your resilience muscle. Being a #Firestarter doesn't come easy. What helps? "Listen to women who have done this already," Tatiana says. Grow from their experiences. "I check in with people that have done this already, and I constantly am listening," she says. "We don't need to reinvent the wheel."

Find some sponsors

Beyond mentors, you need sponsors, Tatiana stresses. A mentor will give you advice; a sponsor will help you pay for the training you need. If you can, be a sponsor yourself.

Get out there and volunteer

You don't have to run for political office to make a difference for causes about which you care. "Social impact is driven by volunteer-ism," Tatiana says. Giving your time or money creates real change. And you can even magnify your impact if your employer matches your donations.

Angie Provost
The Activist

"We belong to the land here."

A #Firestarter's Beginnings

Angie Provost's movement is one that hits close to home for me. *Really* close: Angie and I are cousins, twice removed on my mother's side. Like me, Angie was born in Louisiana, but her path took her to Texas sooner than mine did. She moved from Lafayette to Houston with her family when she was three. As young, single twenty-somethings, we always told Angie that she would grow old in Louisiana. We knew she was destined to marry a Louisiana man.

While she grew up in a big city, it never felt like a fit for her. Angie always considered the Bayou State to be home. "We belong to the land here," she says.

She spent summers there on her grandfather's farm, and she returned to Louisiana when she became engaged to her now-husband, June Provost. June's family has a long history of sugar cane farming, just as hers did, but her grandparents were forced out of farming around the civil rights movement era of the mid-20th century.

"When I met June, I found it so fascinating that his family was still upholding that legacy," Angie says. "I became really involved in studying what he was doing."

The more she learned, the more she felt drawn toward becoming an entrepreneur and being connected to the land, just as June was. She even created her own farm.

Finding Her Fire

But even as Angie and June worked to uphold their families' legacy in agriculture, others were working just as hard to tear it down.

"We really started experiencing some harsh reprisals and harassment," Angie says. They also had to fight back against institutions. They filed a lawsuit, alleging unfair treatment by their bank, and another suit against a prominent local mill for breach of contract.

All of this took a heavy toll on them. June and Angie's home was foreclosed on in September 2018. Angie knew that they were hardly the first farmers of color to go through an ordeal like this. Such treatment had driven her grandparents and many others from their land.

"You love Louisiana, you love the small town, you love the people in it," she says. "But there's very little opportunity and equitable relief if you are a person of color, trying to advance your portfolio or your livelihood."

Amid everything going on, the Provosts were approached with an opportunity that they knew could do good but that was still pretty daunting to consider. A writer asked to tell their story for an article in *The Guardian*, a British daily newspaper with a strong international readership.

"We were afraid to speak up and say what was going on with us," Angie says. They felt victimized, violated and vulnerable, and that was hard to talk about; but they trusted the writer, Debbie Weingarten, and decided to move forward.

The extensive story in *The Guardian* in October 2018 details the Provosts' long nightmare: Vandalized equipment. Surveillance. Dead cats left on a tractor. This will all sound familiar to fans of the television show *Queen Sugar*, which is about a sugarcane farming family. (It's based on a novel by Natalie Baszile, who has become a friend of the Provost family.) But the mistreatment of the Provosts has actually been worse than what was portrayed on the show, Angie says.

After the article appeared, they were nervous. "We didn't know what the response would be," Angie says. But while there have been ups and downs, the article has led to many blessings for them.

"There *are* people out there that there are progressive voices,'" Angie says. "There are those who support change and know that change is for the better for everyone."

After the article, she and June became more active with groups such as the National Family Farm Coalition, National Black Growers Council, and Farm Aid. And they created Provost Farm LLC with the two of them as co-owners.

"The mission of that business is to preserve and advocate for the legacy of African-American sugarcane farmers and black farmers in general," Angie says. "We want people to be aware that, as African Americans, we own less than 1% of rural land in the US. It is steadily declining; it's been declining since Reconstruction."

Angie draws on her deep knowledge of history to put their movement into a larger context. They want to raise awareness of the links between black rural land ownership and other issues, including criminal justice reform, food equity, voter suppression, and redlining.

As they've grown their movement, they've had more opportunities to share their story. The Provosts were even featured in The 1619 Project, a major initiative by *The New York Times* to explore the history and consequences of slavery.

"Participating in The 1619 Project was an honor," Angie says. "June and I believe our voice to be echoes of our ancestors—as if they spoke through us. Their triumphs and defeats but, most of all, their strength. I think what (journalist) Nikole Hannah-Jones has accomplished with *The New York Times* is equivalent to the tales my grandmother told me as a young adult about our family history: the tales that pull you in, paint a picture, and change your life."

Besides fighting for their own livelihood, Angie and June are using their visibility to bring together other black and indigenous farmers in Louisiana and to strengthen their sense of community. They're heartened by the other farmers who are speaking up too—"the sugarcane farmers of the past who want platforms but have lost them."

Spreading Her Spark

Angie knows that she and June are taking on a lot, but that's because they know we're at a critical juncture. "We're in a time where we could either go backward or we could move forward," Angie says.

One way the Provosts are moving forward is by training with the Propeller accelerator program. This New Orleans-based nonprofit supports entrepreneurs who are taking on social and environmental disparities. Propeller found out about the Provosts from *The Guardian* article and reached out to them to participate. Their lead mentor is Richard McCarthy, creator of Crescent City Farmers Market and former director of Slow Food USA. They also plan to travel to Africa to consult with farmers there.

Angie and June see something that others have ignored: a need to tell the story of black farmers in Louisiana in the form of a museum. Propeller is helping Angie and June with plans for a nonprofit that would include a museum or memorial to black farmers. The biggest challenge is securing funding. Angie also envisions an educational center where schoolchildren and others could come and learn more about farming. That's the kind of field trip that I wish I could have taken as a young child. My father's family is from the area Angie and June call home, yet I have never walked the fields that June so often mentions.

"We need to start educating more about rural life and the benefits of maintaining that rural life," she says. That connection with our rural history is vital.

"If you strip someone of their legacy and their history, if you don't educate a community on how that township or area was developed, you're leaving an entire group of people in an insecure position," Angie says. "And that community becomes vulnerable to oppressive tactics."

She knows that there are people who will say "I didn't own slaves" or "I wasn't a slave" and question why we still need to talk about all of this.

"I believe that not talking about your past is a form of insecurity," Angie says. For our future, we must learn from the past and make a better way.

Another way to build a better future is changing laws and policies that hamper farmers of color, Angie says. For example, right now there are too many roadblocks to accessing USDA programs.

"I think these are our right to be a part of," as families who have owned farms for generations, she says. After all, it was people like their ancestors who "taught Europeans how to farm these tropical crops," she points out.

She'd also like to see more actions by groups like the Urban League and the NAACP. "Within our own organizations, we're missing that rural link," she says.

You can help Angie work for change. "Especially if you live in a rural community, you can write to your USDA county committeeman or to your city councilperson," she says. "Ask them what are they doing about farm equity and land loss prevention for people of color." If you can donate money, Angie recommends Farm Aid, which "does a lot for helping the working-class farmer," as well as the National Black Growers Council. Visit www.provostfarmllc.com for a list of other organizations in which you can get involved.

If you are an African American Millennial or Gen-Zer who has rural roots but is living in a big city right now, you could have a vital role to play in Angie's movement. "If your parents own land, if your grandparents own land, make sure that it stays within the family—that you uphold that property," she says. Remember, too, that farming can be a lucrative business. "The reason why it's so difficult for us is because there are so few of us out there." More African Americans becoming active in agriculture equals more strength in numbers.

Although the retaliation and harassment continue, Angie and June are committed to their work because they know they're making a difference.

"I don't want to give the impression that Louisiana is the really despicable state that's not worth living in," she says. It's just that "A lot of us have moved away and the resources aren't here. Let's bring that back. Let's educate people. Let's reform because it's a beautiful place. It's a magical place."

The resolve she shows is in her DNA. "That comes from my grandmother's side of the family," Angie says. "They are some pretty feisty women. We come from a very strong stock of African and Native American heritage. We have a pretty long history, and one of the things that my grandmother, my great-aunt, my great-grandmother have always instilled in us is pride for our legacy and history."

She knows the stories of the women before her, the difficulties they faced, and how they overcame them. She was taught not to be ashamed of facing difficulties but rather to "always move forward and make a way," Angie says. "Those are the things that they instilled in us: a really strong value of family and knowing your past to inform your future."

Ignite Your Own Fire

What can you take away from Angie's story to catalyze your own movement?

Know where you come from

Angie and I both find inspiration in our family history. If you don't know the stories of the people who came before you, now is a great time to ask parents, grandparents, aunts, uncles, and cousins to share their recollections with you. Interview them about how they grew up and the changes they've seen. Don't forget to record those conversations: You'll be forever grateful for that oral history. Whatever you learn from them will shed light on who you are and your unique gifts as a #Firestarter.

Understand your movement's past

Along the same lines, educate yourself about the history of your movement. Part of what sustains Angie is knowing that she's part of something bigger, and no matter what your movement is, so are you. What have others accomplished before you? How can you build on what they've done and honor their legacy?

There's strength in your story

Telling her story in the media has changed Angie's life and advanced her movement. This can feel like a big step, but Angie urges you not to shy away from it if the opportunity arises. "Everyone who tells their story should live in their truth," she says. "Give a real representation to whatever you are trying to change, whatever you are trying to maintain."

Before you get in front of the mic, there are a couple of things Angie wants you to consider: Just make sure the media outlet or any other source you work with is trustworthy and makes you feel comfortable. You also need a community of support around you during what can feel like a vulnerable time.

If you're having trouble mustering the courage to do an interview or to share your story in another way (like writing a blog post), remember that you'll be helping others by doing so.

"When you are a truth teller, when you are a peace speaker, you will find that there are so many people out there that have been waiting to hear your voice," Angie says. "Every single one of us has something to tell. That's why we're here on Earth as human beings. We're here to share our experience and empathize with one another."

Claudia Yoli Ferla
The Dreamer

"I believe in the power of young people and what we can build together and collectively."

A #Firestarter's Beginnings

Claudia Yoli Ferla is a #Firestarter who's all about helping other young women find their fires. She's the co-executive director of Deeds Not Words, an organization founded by former Texas state senator—and current congressional candidate—Wendy Davis. Deeds Not Words teaches young women how to fight for equality and opportunity through organizing, policy-making, art, and voting.

She says that she "would have never in a thousand years" dreamed she would hold a role like her current one, but everything in Claudia's story prepared her for the work she does today.

Claudia was born in Caracas, Venezuela where her mother, Angela, was a lawyer.

"She always practiced the principles of social justice in her work," Claudia says. Sometimes clients would pay her in chickens or eggs. "She always believed in helping the poor and helping the most vulnerable and the most in need."

As political instability grew in Venezuela, Angela decided it was time for her and eight-year-old Claudia to leave. And so they set out for El Paso, Texas where Claudia's two older brothers already lived.

"She came here with a suitcase and a dream," Claudia says.

And Angela wasn't afraid to work hard for that dream. Although she was used to working as a lawyer back in Venezuela, in their new home, she did "everything and anything" to support her family—washing dishes, cooking, waiting tables—you name it.

As hard as she worked, Angela also found the time to give back and contribute to their new community.

I felt a common bond with Claudia who is also Catholic. Her mother taught religious education and volunteered at their church. If you've heard me talk about my family, this holds true for them as well. Angela also volunteered at nonprofits and with Claudia's school, and she was an awesome friend. She banded together with other single mothers to take turns watching each other's kids.

Her mother taught Claudia that "when three people can eat, four can eat." They didn't have much money, but Angela still often invited people over for dinner to share what they had.

As they gave to others, El Paso gave back to them. As Claudia wrote for the website Progress Texas:

> When my mother and I first came to the United States, we were embraced by a community like no other: El Paso, home to desert mountains, mystic sunsets, and vibrant border culture.
>
> I remember making my first friend in America in the playground of an elementary school where your immigration status, your broken English, and the color of your skin didn't matter. A school where so many of us felt safe; welcomed by binational students, bilingual teachers, and bicultural classrooms.
>
> But amid all the wonderful things about Claudia's childhood in El Paso, there was also the shadow of fear. While Angela did go on to get a green card, there was a lot of anxiety before she

did. Claudia and Angela always knew that a single knock on their door could shatter their American dream.

Fast forward to Claudia's teen years. Besides the growing pains all of us experience in adolescence, she had to deal with some serious life transitions and challenges.

The summer before Claudia's senior year in high school, her mother was diagnosed with dementia. Angela and her family decided that the best way for her to get the care she needed would be for her to return to Venezuela. Claudia left her beloved El Paso community to go live with an aunt and uncle in Florida.

"That was really hard for me," she says. Not only was she facing daily life without her mom. She also had to leave behind back in El Paso extracurricular activities about which she was excited.

Also, during her senior year, Claudia finally got an interview for her green card. She went into the interview with reams of glowing recommendations and a school transcript packed with stellar grades. It was to no avail, though. A few days later, she got a letter telling her she had thirty days to leave the country.

But that same day, she also got a very different piece of mail. It was a ticket to a brighter future: an acceptance letter to college. Like her mother, Claudia was determined to fight for that future.

Finding Her Fire

Claudia returned to El Paso to fight the deportation order. Back in the community that raised her, she found plenty of support that fed her resilience.

Thanks to the Deferred Action for Childhood Arrivals (DACA) program, Claudia's deportation case was dismissed. This helped her focus on her education at the University of Texas at El Paso and on discovering who she was as a #Firestarter and a movement-maker.

One of Claudia's pivotal experiences was volunteering for the gubernatorial campaign of Wendy Davis (best known for her thirteen-hour filibuster in the Texas Senate to fight abortion restrictions).

"It taught me how to organize and how to build power in my community, and, most importantly, the power that young people have in changing Texas politics," she says. Davis was not elected governor, and that loss devastated Claudia. But "we won something so much more meaning-ful, which was a generation of fired-up activists."

Claudia went on to serve as a regional field organizer for Texas Freedom Network and director of community affairs for Texas Sen. José Rodríguez. Her career then took her full circle as she joined Deeds Not Words, the nonprofit that Davis founded.

Her first role with the organization was director of student outreach and organizing. She empowered young #Firestarters with the skills they needed to create change.

Now, as co-executive director, she is proud to serve a mission that "even let me get started in the first place: organizing and galvanizing the power of young people."

Claudia has found great power in sharing in her story. She identifies as queer, and when she came out as part of the LGBTQIA community, she was met with support and acceptance in her El Paso community.

But "I think the biggest coming out story was me coming out as undocumented," she says. Although many close to her already knew her immigration status, she made the decision to talk about it publicly after the 2016 presidential election. "Because we knew that no immigrant, whether documented or not, was safe under this administration," she says.

As with her previous coming out experience, she was embraced by her community. She's quick to express her appreciation for those who supported her including the Border Network for Human Rights; Sen. Rodríguez; and Susie Byrd, now the district director for US Rep. Veronica Escobar as well as the larger community of Dreamers.

Spreading Her Spark

Going forward, Claudia wants to keep working for "a change in the rhetoric around immigrant communities." The real story of the border, she says, is "a story of resilience, a story of hope and a story of power."

She adds: "I believe that a lot of it is also a story of young people telling the real story of Texas."

As for how her career as an advocate will unfold, Claudia doesn't have a master plan.

"I'm not in this to build a career," she says. "I'm in this because I'm highly passionate about what I do, and I believe in the power of young people and what we can build together and collectively."

Claudia says that the influence of her mother—who passed away four years after her initial diagnosis—helped her become the #Firestarter she is today and that it will continue to shape her work.

"She always had a very big spirit of community," she says. She inherited that spirit from her mother, and it shapes "the outlook that I have for society and for the world that we live in."

Ignite Your Own Fire

What can you take away from Claudia's story to catalyze your own movement?

Make space for others

Whether you're in a meeting, a training session, or even speaking in a public forum, pause to take a look around you. "Always ask yourself, 'Who isn't here? And why?'" Claudia says. "Make space for those who need to be there." The people who will be most affected by policies need to be able to share their experiences, and the rest of us can uplift and amplify their voices.

Be willing to unlearn

"If we're truly in this work to impact change, we have to also be willing to unlearn," Claudia says. "Unlearn certain behaviors. Unlearn certain preconceived notions, and be willing to understand how they play out in our everyday lives."

Share wisely

"I would tell any young woman, especially young women of color, that their voices matter and that their stories are unique and important to this work," Claudia says. "But only share the stories and the pieces of themselves that they feel comfortable with sharing."

When she first started sharing her own immigration story, Claudia got bombarded with questions and interview requests.

"It can lead to burnout—constantly sharing your trauma," she says. "Saying 'no' is okay. Focusing on yourself and healing is also a really important part of this work."

Fuel Yourself
with Faith and Fortitude

*"What happens to a #Firestarter when the
unthinkable happens? Last year, I found out."*

I thought I knew just what 2019 was going to have in store for me as
a #Firestarter. I had a plan for tackling my master's program in nonprofit leadership at the University of Pennsylvania, writing this book,
continuing my full-time (and very important) lobbyist work, volunteering on community boards, and starting to pitch a TEDx Talk.

Yes, that's a lot. But I told myself I had it. I was good.

But then a sofa came crashing down right in the middle of
all that.

That's not a metaphor.

During a trip to Washington, DC for work, I was enjoying
a reception at one of the Smithsonian Museums. Another guest
lifted a sofa—as in "a large piece of furniture"—to see if their cell
phone was underneath it.

Bad idea, right? Very bad. That sofa fell on my head.

The pain was excruciating, and the diagnosis that unfolded over
the next few days was surreal: I had a traumatic brain injury. I was

lucky I wasn't paralyzed. But I might feel the impact of this injury the rest of my life.

Now *that* gets you to pay attention.

I'm writing this nearly two months after "Night of the Sofa." The concussion I suffered continues to affect my life every day. It's brought me migraines and fatigue. It's made me forgetful and prone to tears.

But that's only one aspect of this experience. Even amid pain, there are gifts. And from chaos and confusion, great clarity can emerge. This experience has changed who I am as a #Firestarter and gifted me with some profound lessons. Those lessons felt like a fitting coda to the other stories of *Find Your Fire*, so I want to close this book by sharing them with you.

First, Repair Yourself

She's so busy taking care of other people that she never pauses to take care of herself.

She's so dedicated. Late nights, every meal at her desk. She's all about the work.

Nothing slows her down. It doesn't matter if she's sick or going through a crisis.

I'm sure you've heard variations of statements like these—maybe in reference to other women, maybe in talking about yourself.

Maybe you've even internalized words like these. Told yourself that being a #Firestarter meant burning yourself down to an ember, all in the name of doing the good you want to do in the world.

Listen. There's nothing like a sofa hitting you in the head to drive home that this ISN'T how things work.

My concussion forced me to reckon with a reality I was slow to acknowledge: Being a #Firestarter means being committed to your physical, emotional, and spiritual health. If you don't tend to them, any movement you start is going to stop cold in its tracks one day.

The fact is that my health was suffering even before I experienced a traumatic brain injury. Before my dad passed away a few years ago, I was fit and at the right weight for me. After losing him, I buried myself in work and in being busy.

I was hiding from grieving, but the pain showed up in my habits and in my body. I moved through life unconsciously. My weight fluctuated and then veered into a territory that made me feel unhealthy.

And in this time of not paying attention, an awful lot of wine sneaked into my life. Now don't get me wrong. I've never worried that I was dependent on alcohol, but a little wine with dinner every night and even a little more wine than that when out with friends adds up.

I had decided to abstain from alcohol for a while even before that sofa came after me, and I absolutely believe it has helped me heal faster.

What else has helped? Movement. I can't do aerobic exercise yet, but just stretching is working wonders for me. I also have a breathing coach. Yes, that's a thing—a thing that's helped me relax and just be more present in this world. It's guiding me toward showing up for some feelings I've been hiding from so I can finally start to work through them.

As I was confronted with the need to take better care of myself, I drew a lot of strength and inspiration from the story of Karen Hansen, one of the fierce #Firestarters behind the brand Wren & Roch. Karen is totally upfront that she could not do the work she does for her fellow survivors without therapy. In the same way, I had to realize that the most important thing I could do for my movement was focus on my own healing.

Taking more time for me means some other things in my life will get less time. It means I can't always say "yes" when people ask me for something. It means I have to limit my contact with people who drain my energy. In a culture that awards us lots of "gold stars" for being busy and always being there for everyone, that's a scary feeling.

But that's a fear I have no choice but to face now, and I couldn't be more grateful.

Freely Give Grace, and Receive It

I don't know what your unique path is, #Firestarter, but I do know this: As you do the work you were put here to do, you will have ample opportunities to both extend and receive grace with yourself and with others. Take them.

As I've healed from this concussion, I've learned that no amount of perfectionism is going to protect me from countless daily annoyances like leaving my phone at home when I go somewhere. This is simply how my injury manifests. I have no control over that. All I can do is grant myself my grace.

In the same way, you won't have control of everything that happens in your movement. Movements are made of humans, and you and the other humans in your movement will mess up sometimes.

I found that out early in my career. One of my proudest achievements is lobbying to turn the Louisiana Smoke-Free Air Act into a law. It restricts smoking in public places like restaurants and makes every workplace smoke-free for all, and it was an unabashed triumph for me and for others who supported the act.

But behind the scenes, things weren't as rosy. In fighting for the act, relationships in our coalition fractured. We were not always nice to each other. Those rifts stayed unhealed for a long time.

When the tenth anniversary of the act's passage came around, I decided to pick up the phone and call a couple of the people from whom I felt most estranged. I apologized, and I thanked them for all they had done.

I could do this because of grace. Grace for them but also grace for myself and the young woman I had been then.

What areas of your life and your movement are crying out for grace right now? For example, if a volunteer doesn't call you back, you could immediately go to a place of resentment and assume she doesn't care about you or your movement anymore, or you could circle back with her and ask if there's something going on in her life with which you could help.

Or what if *you* mess up? I love how #Firestarter Alejandrina Guzman encourages us to stop living in fear of mistakes—because we *are* going to make them. And, as Alejandrina points out, it's not about trying to avoid failure. It's about becoming a person who's really good at bouncing back. That takes giving ourselves abundant grace.

Grace flows from self-awareness and self-reflection—yet another reason you need some stillness even in the midst of your movement. May we all give it generously and receive it gratefully.

Fuel Yourself With Faith and Fortitude

I use these words a lot when I talk about being a #Firestarter and with good reason. My family taught me a master class in the power of faith and fortitude to build movements. I've been drawing strength from that legacy my whole life but never more so than now.

My grandparents have always gone to church every week. And that's how they raised my mother—a woman who still headed for worship an hour before a hurricane was supposed to come through. (But that's another story for another day.)

This is how faith manifested for us in South Louisiana. It is a beautiful but complicated heritage. My ancestors didn't choose their religion. It was imposed on them by slaveholders, but they transformed it into a refuge of faith—one that even today sustains their descendants.

Fortitude is the partner of faith. They fuel each other. My family gave me the fortitude for the work that needed to be done. My grandparents didn't have it easy. They came from sharecroppers. To change things for future generations, my grandfather was a janitor with a side hustle of cleaning offices with his kids at night. My grandmother worked in a school cafeteria. I hear echoes of their lives in the stories that so many women in this book share about their own hard-working families.

Somehow, though, my grandparents also found the fortitude to be present for their community—like when they orchestrated a church raising in their neighborhood when their community desperately needed one.

Times weren't as tight for my parents. My father worked at Exxon, and my mom was a principal. Now if you think that means I didn't have to work for *everything*, well, guess again. When I wanted to go to France on an exchange program in high school, I had to earn the money.

But my family gave me the gift of working alongside me. I helped my grandma make muffuletta sandwiches, and we all sold them to raise money for my trip. That was their love for me and their faith in me in action.

I started talking to God about my head injury and all that it meant for my life even as I sat in the emergency room. As a Christian (in all my imperfections), I am a firm believer that God talks to us in every way. When I got the diagnosis, I actually began to laugh. Not in a snarky way but in the way you laugh when you feel enveloped with comfort. I immediately thought "When God sits you down." And this is what I said:

"I hear you, Lord. I surrender. Please give me patience and grace while you show me the way."

That journey continues. And I continue to pray and to walk every day in faith.

Faith in your life may not look the same way it does in mine. It takes different forms for us all. But whether you find your faith in a house of worship or outside it, through contemplation or through action, the important thing is simply that you have it. What is that spark that ignites you as a #Firestarter? Tend it well.

As you do, surround yourself with people of fortitude. Draw on their wisdom, their belief in you, and their willingness to roll up their sleeves and do the work alongside you. Learn from them.

Let them lift you *and* hold you accountable. My mom knew long before that sofa came after me that I needed to rest more. Now I am actually listening to her. I know that if I hesitate to tell her something during our daily check-ins, that's a good sign that thing is out of alignment with what my priorities are now.

I'm so beyond grateful for her and the other members of my "advisory board" at this pivotal time in my life. We can't go it alone, #Firestarters. We need others, and they need us.

Final Thoughts

I certainly never anticipated getting hit by a sofa and suffering a concussion. (That's putting it mildly!) And I would have never knowingly ventured down this strange stretch of my life path. But as I set out on it, it helped me immeasurably to have the #Firestarter stories you've read in this book fresh in my mind. These women remind me that #Firestarters are not forged by ease and convenience. They spark to life when they face loss; adversity; mistreatment; and, yes, even a flying couch. They turn any obstacle into fuel for their movement.

That's my daily goal, and I hope that's how you're feeling now too. We're in this together, #Firestarters, and together our light will only grow.

FIRESTARTER
TOOLKIT

Firestarter Toolkit

Fuel for Firestarters

Maya Angelou said, "Nothing will work unless you do."

Now that you've heard the stories of some amazing #Firestarters, I hope that you are ready to do some work. In this section, you'll get some of the worksheets and tools that I present during my training, strategy, and coaching sessions and talks. You can use these tools as a starting place to begin your movement and to hold yourself accountable to your vision over time.

Remember, I'm always here to help you go deeper in your work through my webinars, talks, coaching sessions, trainings, and strategy sessions. You'll see my latest offerings at www.terribwilliams.com. In the meantime, you got this!

The Firestarter Formula

Anyone can be a great leader and start a movement! I hope that is one thing that is clear after reading this book. Your movement can be as big as passing a law or building a church or as small as starting a toiletry drive for the homeless.

No matter what your movement is, you need three things:

1. Faith.

2. Fortitude.

3. The Firestarter Formula I'm about to show you.

So what is the Firestarter Formula?

It's simple yet powerful:

- Find the *Cause.*

- *Connect* to build a community or coalition.

- *Communicate* your vision.

- Work to see *Change.*

Ready to use this formula to map out your movement?

Find a Cause

*"It's not enough for us to talk about problems.
We've got to be a part of the solution."*

Amanda Edwards, Chapter 8

You must fully understand what you'd like to change and be able to explain it in a measurable way.

For example:

I am a leader building a movement to eradicate food deserts.

To find and refine your cause, think about questions like these:

- Why do you want to create change? You'll want to get this down to one to two sentences and use it as your elevator pitch.

- What are you driving toward? For example, do you want to hold a rally? To change a rule or law? You might need to tweak your goal later down the road, but what does it look like now?

- Why is now the time to begin a movement in this area? Prove to yourself (and others) that this is the right time. Has there been a catalyst or an event that makes this moment the right one?

- Who will benefit from your movement? By putting a face on your beneficiaries, you'll be more convincing to others and better able to enlist their support.

- Have you pulled together research? You need facts to explain the impact of the problem you're targeting and to show why your plan to solve this problem will work.

- What is the economic case that you will sell to decision-makers? In some movements, you might need to share how you will save an institution money by creating a change.

- What are the pain-points or the speed bumps you must overcome? Be honest with yourself and think through what might stop you from winning.

Connect with a Community

"I started meeting a whole host of people and seeing how politics changes lives if done the right way."

Tishaura Jones, Chapter 11

No leader builds a movement alone. It takes a community. Going back to our food desert example, there are so many people who could step up—from neighbors to grocery store owners to obesity prevention advocates and even kids!

To galvanize a community around your movement, consider these questions:

- Who is a part of your community? Will you build a coalition? You'll know the time is right to build a coalition when other organizations begin to ask you to join your movement.

- Will the beneficiaries of your movement contribute to the work? Your movement will improve the lives of a community. Are they part of the work? This is a good place to check in and bring them on board.

- Is the group at your table diverse? Remember to include those who represent the issue and those whose voices might not be heard. Your community should have diversity in areas like ethnicity, age, and geography.

- Does your community include inspirational leaders? You need people whom others will want to follow.

- How will you recruit "grassroots" and "grasstops"? Grassroots leaders are those who are passionate and ready to work. Grasstop leaders are already influential in the space and might be opinion leaders or experts.

- What resources are available to you? Where will you meet? Do you have the equipment (for example, laptop computers)? Will organizations give you staff? List everything you have that is an asset.

- Who is already working in this movement? Can you collaborate with them? You'll want to find allies or people who care about the same thing that you do. How can you work together to amplify your movement and avoid duplication?

Communicate Your Vision

"When you are a truth teller, when you are a peace speaker, you will find that there are so many people out there that have been waiting to hear your voice."

Angie Provost, Chapter 13

You'll need to communicate both to the other people within your movement and to the rest of the world to spread awareness about what your movement is doing.

These prompts can help you develop your key messages.

- Who is responsible for doing the communications work?

- When will mobilization begin, and what does it look like? Now that you have a coalition built, you can start outlining a plan. You'll finish this plan in the *Change* section.

- Who can help you raise awareness of your movement? Are they willing to step up and speak out on your behalf? Using our food desert example, celebrity chef Jamie Oliver works on food insecurity issues. Perhaps you could ask him to lend his name. Or think about other local or national trendsetters.

- How will you describe to others what you are fighting for? You need to be able to paint a picture for them so they can feel what they can't see.

- Do you have a communications plan? Grab your calendar and map out some key milestones.

- Do you have spokespeople for social media and press? Draft templates and tools that you will need. Things happen quickly in movements, and the more prepared you are, the less stressed you'll be.

- How will you respond to "dream killers"—those who are against your movement? What will you say when someone threatens to stop you? What is your message?

Work to See the Change

"I'm only at the tip of the iceberg, just learning how I can help more people and in the right way and in the most effective way."

Monica Kang, Chapter 4

Now it's time to get in the trenches!

Fine-tune your goal. For example, maybe you've realized through your other prep work that it will be faster and more attainable to get a resolution passed before you attempt to change a law.

- What is a good first step toward starting your movement, and when do you want that first step to occur?

- How will you measure your success? A couple of examples: "We will hold a rally that five hundred people attend." "I will pass a law that will have an impact on five hundred thousand people in my state."

- How will you know you're on or off track? List out some benchmarks to hold yourself accountable.

- How will you celebrate successes? We must always celebrate. Even if you fail, you can always celebrate that you started. We do get an A for effort, #Firestarters.

The Biggest Takeaway

There is one thing that you must remember when using this formula, #Firestarter: Change doesn't end with one action. There's no beginning and end. It doesn't work that way.

Let's say you pass a law like the one that I did to make all restaurants smoke-free. After you pass that law, you have to ensure it's being implemented, meaning the government is putting into place what is in the law. Then you have to make sure the restaurants are following the law; we call that enforcement. There are your dream killers to worry about—those folks that oppose your cause and want to stop you. Well, you have to monitor them to make sure they're not changing the law you passed.

Your biggest takeaway is that there is always work to do, and that's why I made the formula a circle—to remind you the cycle doesn't stop. Stay vigilant and never give up.

Want to Learn More?

I cover each part of the Firestarter Formula in more depth during my trainings, strategy and coaching sessions, and talks.

Motivation Map

I'm so grateful that you've bought my book and read all the way to the end. Wow, you're committed! And for that, I think you need a prize.

If you go to www.terribwilliams.com and the page called Find Your Fire, click the link for your free downloadable Motivation Map.

This is the real gut check for you as a leader who wants to turn a moment into a movement.

Use this tool to map out your motivations for starting your movement. Think of someone like your grandmother or a funder to whom you would explain this work, then write out a description of your movement, why you feel compelled to do this work, and why you need to be the leader of the movement. Then pick three data points that would persuade them to join your movement. Finally, write out one last time why your movement is important.

Commit

Before I let you go, #Firestarter, I want to share my favorite quote from Peter Pan: "Nothing is really work unless you would rather be doing something else."

When you're in the thick of your movement, time and space won't matter. You'll forget to eat. You won't feel the sweat rolling down your back, and you'll ignore your phone. It's all because you've been moved to lead a change, to start something others have ignored. This moment is yours, and it is time to own it!

All it takes to change the world is one person doing one thing. Now it is time to commit to yourself that you're ready to do the work and succeed. You're on fire! And you're made for this very moment.

No one else that can do this work with your heart, intention, and work ethic. Listen to your gut, attract the right partners, communicate your desire to create change, and you will find the courage you need in every situation. Now pick up a pen and pinkie swear to yourself that a successful movement is on the way!

I, _____ (your name), am a leader who will turn a moment into a movement. I care about this cause: _____(movement name).

I will communicate this with _____ (accountability partner) because I want to see a change in _____ _____ (name of community or field).

I will take the following three steps to start my movement:

1. _____
2. _____
3. _____

I promise to unleash my full potential by doing these three things to keep myself on track:

1. _____
2. _____
3. _____

When my movement is at its peak or complete, I will celebrate by _____ (activity) because I know I have improved the lives of _____.

With faith and fortitude, I will find a way to make it happen because I am a #Firestarter.

Signed _____
Date _____

Firestarter Formula with Faith and Fortitude

A Personal Formula to Begin
Your Movement Within

#FindYourFire

cause	
collective	
communicate	
change	
COMMIT	

Movement Motivation Map

What Drives You, #Firestarter?

Use this tool to map out your motivations for starting your movement. Think of someone like your grandmother or funder that you would explain this work to. Then write out a description of your movement, why you feel compelled to do this work and why you need to be the leader of the movement. Then pick three data points that would persuade them to join your movement. Finally, write out one last time why your movement is important.

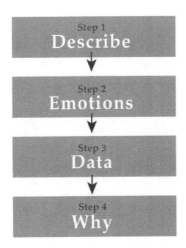

Describe	
Emotions	
Data	
Why	

About the Author

Terri Broussard Williams believes leaders turn moments into movements. Throughout her accomplished career as an author, broadcast journalist, press secretary for a US Senate Candidate, philanthropist, and lobbyist, Williams has turned public and community service into a professional art-form that has positively impacted millions of lives. For nearly sixteen years, Terri made the American Heart Association (AHA) her career home. Her journey at this notable organization sparked her dream of creating significant, community-shifting outcomes. She counts some of the pieces of legislation passed as some of her most distinguished accomplishments, including the Louisiana Smoke-Free Air Act, a game-changing career milestone she experienced at the flourishing age of twenty-eight. Broussard Williams received her bachelor's degree from Louisiana State University and is also a graduate of the Social Impact Strategy Executive Education Program at the University of Pennsylvania and holds a graduate certificate in diversity and inclusion from Cornell University. She is an honors graduate of The University of Pennsylvania with a master's degree in Non Profit Leadership, and she received the Excellence in Social Impact Strategy award at graduation. Terri was fortunate to serve as a student commencement speaker at her graduation. She has served on several boards including the Austin Area Urban League, the Annette Strauss Institute for Civic Engagement, the University of Texas McCombs School of Business Capstone Advisory Board, Louisiana State University National Diversity Advisory Board, and the Association of Junior

Leagues International among others. In addition to her day job as a tech lobbyist, Terri is focused on paying it forward—using her blog, MovementMakerCollective.com, to encourage and build up others who strive to create meaningful and ground-breaking change. Get to know more about this #firestarter at terribwilliams.com.

IT'S YOUR TIME

OWN IT

Made in the USA
Middletown, DE
23 November 2020